Scholars Praise Śrī Īśopaniṣad

"The eighteen Sanskrit *mantras* of *Śrī Īśopaniṣad* are given in both *devanāgari* and roman script, something that will be of great help to the beginning student. Swami Prabhupāda has given intelligent and lucid commentaries on every *mantra,* and—unusual for this type of publication—a glossary and index have been added."

Dr. Paul Hockings
Professor of Anthropology
University of Illinois

"The first available English edition of *Śrī Īśopaniṣad* makes this most significant publication accessible to a broader public of students and scholars. This spiritual lawbook, with a most useful introduction by His Divine Grace A.C. Bhaktivedanta Swami Prabhupāda, is a necessary supplement to any serious study of the Vedic culture. The Sanskrit diacritical equivalents and the glossary are most useful guides to further study and deeper understanding of ancient spiritual law and Vedic culture.

"I recommend this volume to any student or scholar of Vedic thought. To the generalist and specialist alike it will generate considerable provocation and understanding. It is an indispensable addition to any serious library collection."

Dr. Thomas N. Pappas
Professor of History
Anderson College

श्री ईशोपनिषद्

ŚRĪ ĪŚOPANIṢAD

BOOKS by His Divine Grace
A. C. Bhaktivedanta Swami Prabhupāda

Bhagavad-gītā As It Is
Śrīmad-Bhāgavatam, Cantos 1–10 (12 volumes)
Śrī Caitanya-caritāmṛta (17 volumes)
Teachings of Lord Caitanya
The Nectar of Devotion
Śrī Īśopaniṣad
The Nectar of Instruction
Easy Journey to Other Planets
Kṛṣṇa, the Supreme Personality of Godhead
Perfect Questions, Perfect Answers
The Path of Perfection
Teachings of Queen Kuntī
The Science of Self-Realization
Dialectical Spiritualism
The Journey of Self-Discovery
A Second Chance
Conversations with Śrīla Prabhupāda (37 volumes)
Śrī Śikṣāmṛta (letters, 3 volumes)
Collected Lectures on Śrīmad-Bhāgavatam (11 volumes)
Collected Lectures on Bhagavad-gītā (7 volumes)
Kṛṣṇa Consciousness: The Topmost Yoga System
Teachings of Lord Kapila, the Son of Devahūti
Search for Liberation
Life Comes from Life
The Perfection of Yoga
Beyond Birth and Death
On the Way to Kṛṣṇa
Message of Godhead
The Laws of Nature: An Infallible Justice
Civilization and Transcendence
Renunciation Through Wisdom
Rāja-vidyā: The King of Knowledge
Elevation to Kṛṣṇa Consciousness
Kṛṣṇa Consciousness: The Matchless Gift
Nārada-bhakti-sūtra (with disciples)
Mukunda-mālā-stotra (with disciples)
Back to Godhead magazine (founder)
Geetār-gān (Bengali)
Bhakti-ratna-boli (Bengali)

A complete catalog is available upon request.

In North America:
The Bhaktivedanta Book Trust
3764 Watseka Avenue
Los Angeles, California 90034

In Australasia:
The Bhaktivedanta Book Trust
P.O. Box 262
Botany, N.S.W., Australia

ŚRĪ ĪŚOPANIṢAD

The Knowledge That Brings One Nearer to
The Supreme Personality of Godhead, Kṛṣṇa

With introduction, translation
and authorized purports by

HIS DIVINE GRACE
A. C. Bhaktivedanta Swami Prabhupāda
Founder-*Ācārya* of the International Society
For Krishna Consciousness

THE BHAKTIVEDANTA BOOK TRUST
Los Angeles • London • Stockholm • Bombay • Sydney • Hong Kong

THE COVER: Beauty, mystery, and unlimited power unite in the form of the Lord, the *Īśa* in *Īśopaniṣad*. Here He is depicted as Śrī Keśava, one of the Viṣṇu expansions of Kṛṣṇa, the Supreme Personality of Godhead.

Readers interested in the subject matter of this book are invited by the International Society for Krishna Consciousness to correspond with its secretary at one of the following addresses:

International Society for Krishna Consciousness
3764 Watseka Avenue
Los Angeles, California 90034
USA
Telephone: 1-800-927-4152

International Society for Krishna Consciousness
P. O. Box 262
Botany
N.S.W. 2019
Australia

Twelfth printing, 1993: 150,000
Thirteenth printing, 1995: 150,000

Printed in the United States of America

Library of Congress Cataloging-in-Publication Data

Upanishads. Īśopaniṣad. English.
Śrī Īśopaniṣad : the knowledge that brings one nearer to the supreme personality of Godhead, Kṛṣṇa ; with introduction, translation, and authorized purports / by A. C. Bhaktivedanta Swami Prabhupāda.
p. cm.
Includes index.
ISBN 0-89213-280-9
I. A. C. Bhaktivedanta Swami Prabhupāda, 1896–1977. II. Title.
BL1124.7.I762E5 1993
294.5'9218—dc20 93-15792
CIP

Contents

Introduction

"Teachings of the *Vedas*"

(Delivered as a lecture by His Divine Grace A. C. Bhaktivedanta Swami Prabhupāda on October 6, 1969, at Conway Hall, London, England.)

Ladies and gentlemen, today's subject matter is the teachings of the *Vedas.* What are the *Vedas*? The Sanskrit verbal root of *veda* can be interpreted variously, but the purport is finally one. *Veda* means knowledge. Any knowledge you accept is *veda,* for the teachings of the *Vedas* are the original knowledge. In the conditioned state, our knowledge is subjected to many deficiencies. The difference between a conditioned soul and a liberated soul is that the conditioned soul has four kinds of defects. The first defect is that he must commit mistakes. For example, in our country, Mahatma Gandhi was considered to be a very great personality, but he committed many mistakes. Even at the last stage of his life, his assistant warned, "Mahatma Gandhi, don't go to the New Delhi meeting. I have some friends, and I have heard there is danger." But he did not hear. He persisted in going and was killed. Even great personalities like Mahatma Gandhi, President Kennedy—there are so many of them—make mistakes. To err is human. This is one defect of the conditioned soul.

Another defect: to be illusioned. Illusion means to accept something which is not: *māyā. Māyā* means "what is not." Everyone is accepting the body as the self. If I ask you what you are, you will say, "I am Mr. John; I am a rich man; I am this; I am that." All these are bodily identifications. But you are not this body. This is illusion.

The third defect is the cheating propensity. Everyone has the propensity to cheat others. Although a person is fool number one, he poses himself as very intelligent. Although it is already pointed out that he is in illusion and makes mistakes, he will theorize: "I think this is this, this is this." But he does not even know his own position. He writes books of philosophy, although he is defective. That is his disease. That is cheating.

Lastly, our senses are imperfect. We are very proud of our eyes. Often, someone will challenge, "Can you show me God?" But do you have the eyes to see God? You will never see if you haven't the eyes. If immediately the room becomes dark, you cannot even see your hands. So what power do you have to see? We cannot, therefore, expect knowledge (*veda*) with these imperfect senses. With all these deficiencies, in conditioned life we cannot give perfect knowledge to anyone. Nor are we ourselves perfect. Therefore we accept the *Vedas* as they are.

You may call the *Vedas* Hindu, but "Hindu" is a

foreign name. We are not Hindus. Our real identification is *varṇāśrama. Varṇāśrama* denotes the followers of the *Vedas,* those who accept the human society in eight divisions of *varṇa* and *āśrama.* There are four divisions of society and four divisions of spiritual life. This is called *varṇāśrama.* It is stated in the *Bhagavad-gītā* [4.13], "These divisions are everywhere because they are created by God." The divisions of society are *brāhmaṇa, kṣatriya, vaiśya, śūdra. Brāhmaṇa* refers to the very intelligent class of men, those who know what is Brahman. Similarly, the *kṣatriyas,* the administrator group, are the next intelligent class of men. Then the *vaiśyas,* the mercantile group. These natural classifications are found everywhere. This is the Vedic principle, and we accept it. Vedic principles are accepted as axiomatic truth, for there cannot be any mistake. That is acceptance. For instance, in India cow dung is accepted as pure, and yet cow dung is the stool of an animal. In one place you'll find the Vedic injunction that if you touch stool, you have to take a bath immediately. But in another place it is said that the stool of a cow is pure. If you smear cow dung in an impure place, that place becomes pure. With our ordinary sense we can argue, "This is contradictory." Actually, it is contradictory from the ordinary point of view, but it is not false. It is fact. In Calcutta, a very prominent scientist and doctor analyzed cow dung and found that it contains all antiseptic properties.

In India if one person tells another, "You must do this," the other party may say, "What do you mean? Is this a Vedic injunction, that I have to follow you without any argument?" Vedic injunctions cannot be interpreted. But ultimately, if you carefully study why these injunctions are there, you will find that they are all correct.

The *Vedas* are not compilations of human knowledge. Vedic knowledge comes from the spiritual world, from Lord Kṛṣṇa. Another name for the *Vedas* is *śruti*. *Śruti* refers to that knowledge which is acquired by hearing. It is not experimental knowledge. *Śruti* is considered to be like a mother. We take so much knowledge from our mother. For example, if you want to know who your father is, who can answer you? Your mother. If the mother says, "Here is your father," you have to accept it. It is not possible to experiment to find out whether he is your father. Similarly, if you want to know something beyond your experience, beyond your experimental knowledge, beyond the activities of the senses, then you have to accept the *Vedas*. There is no question of experimenting. It has already been experimented. It is already settled. The version of the mother, for instance, has to be accepted as truth. There is no other way.

The *Vedas* are considered to be the mother, and Brahmā is called the grandfather, the forefather, because he was the first to be instructed in the Vedic knowledge. In the beginning the first living creature was Brahmā. He received this Vedic knowledge and imparted it to Nārada and other disciples and sons, and they also distributed it to their disciples. In this way, the Vedic knowledge comes down by disciplic succession. It is also confirmed in the *Bhagavad-gītā* that Vedic knowledge is understood in this way. If you make experimental endeavor, you come to the same conclusion, but just to save time you should accept. If you want to know who your father is and if you accept your mother as the authority, then whatever she says can be accepted without argument. There are three kinds of evidence: *pratyakṣa, anumāna* and *śabda. Pratyakṣa* means "direct evidence." Direct evidence is not very good because our senses are not perfect. We are seeing the sun daily, and it appears to us just like a small disc, but it is actually far, far larger than many planets. Of what value is this seeing? Therefore we have to read books; then we can understand about the sun. So direct experience is not perfect. Then there is *anumāna,* inductive knowledge: "It may be like this"—hypothesis. For instance, Darwin's theory says it may be like this, it may be like that. But that is not science. That is a suggestion, and it is also not perfect. But if you receive the knowledge from the authoritative sources, that is perfect. If you receive a program guide from the radio station authorities, you accept it. You don't deny it; you don't have to make an experiment, because it is received from the authoritative sources.

Vedic knowledge is called *śabda-pramāṇa.* Another name is *śruti. Śruti* means that this knowledge has to be received simply by aural reception. The *Vedas* instruct that in order to understand transcendental knowledge, we have to hear from the authority. Transcendental knowledge is knowledge from beyond this universe. Within this universe is material knowledge, and beyond this universe is transcendental knowledge. We cannot even go to the end of the universe, so how can we go to the spiritual world? Thus to acquire full knowledge is impossible.

There is a spiritual sky. There is another nature, which is beyond manifestation and nonmanifestation. But how will you know that there is a sky where the planets and inhabitants are eternal? All this knowledge is there, but how will you make experiments? It is not possible. Therefore you have to take the assistance of the *Vedas*. This is called Vedic knowledge. In our Kṛṣṇa consciousness movement we are accepting knowledge from the highest authority, Kṛṣṇa. Kṛṣṇa is accepted as the highest authority by all classes of men. I am speaking first of the two classes of transcendentalists. One class of transcendentalists is called impersonalistic, Māyāvādī. They are generally known as Vedāntists, led by Śaṅkarācārya. And there is another class of transcendentalists, called Vaiṣṇavas, like Rāmānujācārya, Madhvācārya, Viṣṇusvāmī. Both the Śaṅkara-sampradāya and the Vaiṣṇava-sampradāya have accepted Kṛṣṇa as the Supreme Personality of Godhead. Śaṅkarācārya is supposed to be an impersonalist who preached impersonalism, impersonal Brahman, but it is a fact that he is a covered personalist. In his commentary on the *Bhagavad-gītā* he wrote, "Nārāyaṇa, the Supreme Personality of Godhead, is beyond this cosmic manifestation." And then again he confirmed, "That Supreme Personality of Godhead, Nārāyaṇa, is Kṛṣṇa. He has come as the son of Devakī and Vasudeva." He particularly mentioned the names of His father and mother. So Kṛṣṇa is accepted as the Supreme Personality of Godhead by all transcendentalists. There is no doubt about it. Our source of knowledge in Kṛṣṇa consciousness is the *Bhagavad-gītā,* which comes directly from Kṛṣṇa. We have published the

Bhagavad-gītā As It Is because we accept Kṛṣṇa as He is speak-ing, without any interpretation. That is Vedic knowl-edge. Since the Vedic knowledge is pure, we accept it. Whatever Kṛṣṇa says, we accept. This is Kṛṣṇa consciousness. That saves much time. If you accept the right authority, or source of knowl-edge, then you save much time. For example, there are two systems of knowledge in the material world: inductive and deductive. From deductive, you accept that man is mortal. Your father says man is mortal, your sister says man is mortal, everyone says man is mortal—but you do not experiment. You accept it as a fact that man is mortal. If you want to research to find out whether man is mortal, you have to study each and every man, and you may come to think that there may be some man who is not dying but you have not seen him yet. So in this way your research will never be finished. In Sanskrit this process is called *āroha,* the ascending process. If you want to attain knowledge by any personal endeavor, by exercising your imperfect senses, you will never come to the right conclusions. That is not possible.

There is a statement in the *Brahma-saṁhitā:* Just ride on the airplane which runs at the speed of mind. Our material airplanes can run two thousand miles per hour, but what is the speed of mind? You are sitting at home, you immediately think of India—say, ten thousand miles away—and at once it is in your home. Your mind has gone there. The mind-speed is so swift. Therefore it is stated, "If you travel at this speed for millions of years, you'll find that the spiritual sky is unlimited." It is not possible even to approach it. Therefore, the Vedic injunction is that one must approach—the word "compulsory" is used—a bona fide spiritual master, a *guru.* And what is the qualification of a spiritual master? He is one who has rightly heard the Vedic message from the right source. And he must practically be firmly established in Brahman. These are the two qualities. Otherwise he is not bona fide.

This Kṛṣṇa consciousness movement is completely authorized from Vedic principles. In the *Bhagavad-gītā* Kṛṣṇa says, "The actual aim of Vedic research is to find out Kṛṣṇa." In the *Brahma-saṁhitā* it is also stated, "Kṛṣṇa, Govinda, has innumerable forms, but they are all one." They are not like our forms, which are fallible. His form is infallible. My form has a beginning, but His form has no beginning. It is *ananta.* And His form—so many multiforms—has no end. My form is sitting here and not in my apartment. You are sitting there and not in your apartment. But Kṛṣṇa can be everywhere at one time. He can sit down in Goloka Vṛndāvana, and at the same time He is everywhere, all-pervading. He is original, the oldest, but whenever you look at a picture of Kṛṣṇa you'll find a young boy fifteen or twenty years old. You will never find an old man. You have seen pictures of Kṛṣṇa as a charioteer from the *Bhagavad-gītā.* At that time He was not less than one hundred years old. He had great-grandchildren, but He looked just like a boy. Kṛṣṇa, God, never becomes old. That is His supreme power. And if you want to search out Kṛṣṇa by studying the Vedic literature, then you will be baffled. It may be possible, but it is very difficult. But you can very easily learn about Him from His devotee. His devotee can deliver Him to you: "Here He is, take Him." That is the potency of Kṛṣṇa's devotees.

Originally there was only one *Veda,* and there was no necessity of reading it. People were so intelligent and had such sharp memories that by once hearing from the lips of the spiritual master they would understand. They would immediately grasp the whole purport. But five thousand years ago Vyāsadeva put the *Vedas* in writing for the people in this age, Kali-yuga. He knew that eventually the people would be short-lived, their memories would be very poor, and their intelligence would not be very sharp. "Therefore, let me teach this Vedic knowledge in writing." He divided the *Vedas* into four: *Ṛg, Sāma, Atharva* and *Yajur.* Then he gave the charge of these *Vedas* to his different disciples. He then thought of the less intelligent class of men—*strī, śūdra* and *dvija-bandhu.* He considered the woman class and *śūdra* class (worker class) and *dvija-bandhu. Dvija-bandhu* refers to those who are born in a high family but who are not properly qualified. A man who is born in the family of a *brāhmaṇa* but is not qualified as a *brāhmaṇa* is called *dvija-bandhu.* For these persons he compiled the *Mahābhārata,* called the history of India, and the eighteen *Purāṇas.* These are all part of the Vedic literature: the *Purāṇas*, the *Mahābhārata,* the four *Vedas* and the *Upaniṣads.* The *Upaniṣads* are part of the *Vedas.* Then Vyāsadeva summarized all Vedic knowledge for scholars and philosophers in what is called the *Vedānta-sūtra.* This is the last word of the *Vedas.*

Vyāsadeva personally wrote the *Vedānta-sūtra* under the instructions of Nārada, his Guru Mahārāja (spiritual master), but still he was not satisfied. That is a long story, described in *Śrīmad-Bhāgavatam.* Vedavyāsa was not very satisfied even after compiling many *Purāṇas* and *Upaniṣads*, and even after writing the *Vedānta-sūtra.* Then his spiritual master, Nārada, instructed him, "You explain the *Vedānta-sūtra.*" *Vedānta* means "ultimate knowledge," and the ultimate knowledge is Kṛṣṇa. Kṛṣṇa says that throughout all the *Vedas* one has to understand Him: *vedānta-kṛd veda-vid eva cāham.* Kṛṣṇa says, "I am the compiler of the *Vedānta-sūtra,* and I am the knower of the *Vedas.*" Therefore the ultimate objective is Kṛṣṇa. That is explained in all the Vaiṣṇava commentaries on *Vedānta* philosophy. We Gauḍīya Vaiṣṇavas have our commentary on *Vedānta* philosophy, called *Govinda-bhāṣya,* by Baladeva Vidyābhūṣaṇa. Similarly, Rāmānujācārya has a commentary, and Madhvācārya has one. The version of Śaṅkarācārya is not the only commentary. There are many *Vedānta* commentaries, but because the Vaiṣṇavas did not present the first *Vedānta* commentary, people are under the wrong impression that Śaṅkarācārya's is the only *Vedānta* commentary. Besides that, Vyāsadeva himself wrote the perfect *Vedānta* commentary, *Śrīmad-Bhāgavatam. Śrīmad-Bhāgavatam* begins with the first words of the *Vedānta-sūtra: janmādy asya yataḥ.* And that *janmādy asya yataḥ* is fully explained in *Śrīmad-Bhāgavatam.* The *Vedānta-sūtra* simply hints at what is Brahman, the Absolute Truth: "The Absolute Truth is that from whom everything emanates." This is a summary, but it is explained in detail in *Śrīmad-Bhāgavatam.* If everything is emanating from the

Absolute Truth, then what is the nature of the Absolute Truth? That is explained in *Śrīmad-Bhāgavatam.* The Absolute Truth must be consciousness. He is self-effulgent (*sva-rāṭ*). We develop our consciousness and knowledge by receiving knowledge from others, but for Him it is said that He is self-effulgent. The whole summary of Vedic knowledge is the *Vedānta-sūtra,* and the *Vedānta-sūtra* is explained by the writer himself in *Śrīmad-Bhāgavatam.* We finally request those who are actually after Vedic knowledge to try to understand the explanation of all Vedic knowledge from *Śrīmad-Bhāgavatam* and the *Bhagavad-gītā.*

Invocation

ॐ पूर्णमदः पूर्णमिदं पूर्णात् पूर्णमुदच्यते ।
पूर्णस्य पूर्णमादाय पूर्णमेवावशिष्यते ॥

oṁ pūrṇam adaḥ pūrṇam idaṁ
pūrṇāt pūrṇam udacyate
pūrṇasya pūrṇam ādāya
pūrṇam evāvaśiṣyate

oṁ—the Complete Whole; *pūrṇam*—perfectly complete; *adaḥ*—that; *pūrṇam*—perfectly complete; *idam*—this phenomenal world; *pūrṇāt*—from the all-perfect; *pūrṇam*—complete unit; *udacyate*—is produced; *pūrṇasya*—of the Complete Whole; *pūrṇam*—completely, all; *ādāya*—having been taken away; *pūrṇam*—the complete balance; *eva*—even; *avaśiṣyate*—is remaining.

TRANSLATION

The Personality of Godhead is perfect and complete, and because He is completely perfect, all emanations from Him, such as this phenomenal world, are perfectly equipped as complete wholes. Whatever is produced of the Complete Whole is also complete in itself. Because He is the Complete Whole, even though so many complete units emanate from Him, He remains the complete balance.

PURPORT

The Complete Whole, or the Supreme Absolute Truth, is the complete Personality of Godhead. Realization of impersonal Brahman or of Paramātmā, the Supersoul, is incomplete realization of the Absolute Complete. The Supreme Personality of Godhead is *sac-cid-ānanda-vigraha.* Realization of impersonal Brahman is realization of His *sat* feature, or His aspect of eternity, and Paramātmā realization is realization of His *sat* and *cit* features, His aspects of eternity and knowledge. But realization of the Personality of Godhead is realization of all the transcendental features—*sat, cit* and *ānanda,* bliss. When one realizes the Supreme Person, he realizes these aspects of the Absolute Truth in their completeness. *Vigraha* means "form." Thus the Complete Whole is not formless. If He were formless, or if He were less than His creation in any other way, He could not be complete. The Complete Whole must contain everything both within and beyond our experience; otherwise He cannot be complete.

The Complete Whole, the Personality of Godhead, has immense potencies, all of which are as complete as He is. Thus this phenomenal world is also complete in itself. The twenty-four elements of which this material universe is a temporary manifestation are arranged to produce everything necessary for the maintenance and subsistence of this universe. No other unit in the universe need make an extraneous effort to try to maintain the universe. The universe functions on its own time scale, which is fixed by the energy of the Complete Whole, and when that schedule is completed, this temporary manifestation will be annihilated by the complete arrangement of the Complete Whole.

All facilities are given to the small complete units (namely the living beings) to enable them to realize the Complete Whole. All forms of incompleteness are experienced due to incomplete knowledge of the Complete Whole. The human form of life is a complete manifestation of the consciousness of the living being, and it is obtained after evolving through 8,400,000 species of life in the cycle of birth and death. If in this human life of full consciousness the living entity does not realize his completeness in relation to the Complete Whole, he loses the chance to realize his completeness and is again put into the evolutionary cycle by the law of material nature.

Because we do not know that there is a complete arrangement in nature for our maintenance, we make efforts to utilize the resources of nature to create a so-called complete life of sense enjoyment. Because the living entity cannot enjoy the life of the senses without being dovetailed with the Complete Whole, the misleading life of sense enjoyment is illusion. The hand of a body is a complete unit only as long as it is attached to the complete body. When the hand is severed from the body, it may appear like a hand, but it actually has none of the potencies of a hand. Similarly, living beings are part and parcel of the Complete Whole, and if they are severed from the Complete Whole, the illusory representation of completeness cannot fully satisfy them.

The completeness of human life can be realized only when one engages in the service of the Complete Whole. All services in this world—whether social, political, communal, international or even interplanetary—will remain incomplete until they are dovetailed with the Complete Whole. When everything is dovetailed with the Complete Whole, the attached parts and parcels also become complete in themselves.

Mantra One

ईशावास्यमिदꣳ सर्वं यत्किञ्च जगत्यां जगत् ।
तेन त्यक्तेन भुञ्जीथा मा गृधः कस्य स्विद् धनम् ॥ १ ॥

īśāvāsyam idaṁ sarvaṁ
yat kiñca jagatyāṁ jagat
tena tyaktena bhuñjīthā
mā gṛdhaḥ kasya svid dhanam

īśa—by the Lord; *āvāsyam*—controlled; *idam*—this; *sarvam*—all; *yat kiñca*—whatever; *jagatyām*—within the universe; *jagat*—all that is animate or inanimate; *tena*—by Him; *tyaktena*—set-apart quota; *bhuñjīthāḥ*—you should accept; *mā*—do not; *gṛdhaḥ*—endeavor to gain; *kasya svit*—of anyone else; *dhanam*—the wealth.

TRANSLATION

Everything animate or inanimate that is within the universe is controlled and owned by the Lord. One should therefore accept only those things necessary for himself, which are set aside as his quota, and one should not accept other things, knowing well to whom they belong.

PURPORT

Vedic knowledge is infallible because it comes down

through the perfect disciplic succession of spiritual masters, beginning with the Lord Himself. Since He spoke the first word of Vedic knowledge, the source of this knowledge is transcendental. The words spoken by the Lord are called *apauruṣeya,* which indicates that they are not delivered by any mundane person. A living being who lives in the mundane world has four defects: (1) he is certain to commit mistakes; (2) he is subject to illusion; (3) he has a propensity to cheat others; and (4) his senses are imperfect. No one with these four imperfections can deliver perfect knowledge. The *Vedas* are not produced by such an imperfect creature. Vedic knowledge was originally imparted by the Lord into the heart of Brahmā, the first created living being, and Brahmā in his turn disseminated this knowledge to his sons and disciples, who have handed it down through history.

Since the Lord is *pūrṇam,* all-perfect, there is no possibility of His being subjected to the laws of material nature, which He controls. However, both the living entities and inanimate objects are controlled by the laws of nature and ultimately by the Lord's potency. This *Īśopaniṣad* is part of the *Yajur Veda,* and consequently it contains information concerning the proprietorship of all things existing within the universe.

The Lord's proprietorship over everything within the universe is confirmed in the Seventh Chapter of the *Bhagavad-gītā* (7.4–5), where *parā* and *aparā prakṛti* are discussed. The elements of nature—earth, water, fire, air, ether, mind, intelligence and ego—all belong to the Lord's inferior, material energy (*aparā prakṛti*),whereas the living being, the organic energy, is His superior energy (*parā prakṛti*). Both of these *prakṛtis,* or energies, are emanations from the Lord, and ultimately He is the controller of everything that exists. There is nothing in the universe that does not belong either to the *parā* or the *aparā prakṛti;* therefore everything is the property of the Supreme Being.

Because the Supreme Being, the Absolute Personality of Godhead, is the complete person, He has complete and perfect intelligence to adjust everything by means of His different potencies. The Supreme Being is often compared to a fire, and everything organic and inorganic is compared to the heat and light of that fire. Just as fire distributes energy in the form of heat and light, the Lord displays His energy in different ways. He thus remains the ultimate controller, sustainer and dictator of everything. He is the possessor of all potencies, the knower of everything and the benefactor of everyone. He is full of inconceivable opulence, power, fame, beauty, knowledge and renunciation.

One should therefore be intelligent enough to know that except for the Lord no one is a proprietor of anything. One should accept only those things that are set aside by the Lord as his quota. The cow, for instance, gives milk, but she does not drink that milk: she eats grass and straw, and her milk is designated as food for human beings. Such is the arrangement of the Lord. Thus we should be satisfied with those things He has kindly set aside for us, and we should always consider to whom those things we possess actually belong.

Take, for example, our dwelling, which is made of earth, wood, stone, iron, cement and so many other material things. If we think in terms of *Śrī Īśopaniṣad,* we must know that we cannot produce any of these building materials ourselves. We can simply bring them together and transform them into different shapes by our labor. A laborer cannot claim to be a proprietor of a thing just because he has worked hard to manufacture it.

In modern society there is always a great quarrel between the laborers and the capitalists. This quarrel has taken an international shape, and the world is in danger. Men face one another in enmity and snarl just like cats and dogs. *Śrī Īśopaniṣad* cannot give advice to the cats and dogs, but it can deliver the message of Godhead to man through the bona fide *ācāryas* (holy teachers). The human race should take the Vedic wisdom of *Śrī Īśopaniṣad* and not quarrel over material possessions. One must be satisfied with whatever privileges are given to him by the mercy of the Lord. There can be no peace if the communists or capitalists or any other party claims proprietorship over the resources of nature, which are entirely the property of the Lord. The capitalists cannot curb the communists simply by political maneuvering, nor can the communists defeat the capitalists simply by fighting for stolen bread. If they do not recognize the proprietorship of the Supreme Personality of Godhead, all the property they claim to be their own is stolen. Consequently they will be liable to punishment by the laws of nature. Nuclear bombs are in the hands of both communists and capitalists, and if both do not recognize the proprietorship of the Supreme

Lord, it is certain that these bombs will ultimately ruin both parties. Thus in order to save themselves and bring peace to the world, both parties must follow the instructions of *Śrī Īśopaniṣad.*

Human beings are not meant to quarrel like cats and dogs. They must be intelligent enough to realize the importance and aim of human life. The Vedic literature is meant for humanity and not for cats and dogs. Cats and dogs can kill other animals for food without incurring sin, but if a man kills an animal for the satisfaction of his uncontrolled taste buds, he is responsible for breaking the laws of nature. Consequently he must be punished.

The standard of life for human beings cannot be applied to animals. The tiger does not eat rice and wheat or drink cow's milk, because he has been given food in the shape of animal flesh. Among the many animals and birds, some are vegetarian and others are carnivorous, but none of them transgress the laws of nature, which have been ordained by the will of the Lord. Animals, birds, reptiles and other lower life forms strictly adhere to the laws of nature; therefore there is no question of sin for them, nor are the Vedic instructions meant for them. Human life alone is a life of responsibility.

It is wrong, however, to think that simply by becoming a vegetarian one can avoid transgressing the laws of nature. Vegetables also have life, and while it is nature's law that one living being is meant to feed on another, for human beings the point is to recognize the Supreme Lord. Thus one should not be proud of being a strict vegetarian. Animals do not have developed consciousness by which to recognize the Lord, but a human being is sufficiently intelligent to take lessons from the Vedic literature and thereby know how the laws of nature are working and derive profit out of such knowledge. If a man neglects the instructions of the Vedic literature, his life becomes very risky. A human being is therefore required to recognize the authority of the Supreme Lord and become His devotee. He must offer everything for the Lord's service and partake only of the remnants of food offered to the Lord. This will enable him to discharge his duty properly. In the *Bhagavad-gītā* (9.26) the Lord directly states that He accepts vegetarian food from the hands of a pure devotee. Therefore a human being should not only become a strict vegetarian but should also become a devotee of the Lord, offer the Lord all his food and then partake of such *prasādam,* or the mercy of God. Only those who act in this way can properly discharge the duties of human life. Those who do not offer their food to the Lord eat nothing but sin and subject themselves to various types of distress, which are the results of sin (Bg. 3.13).

The root of sin is deliberate disobedience of the laws of nature through disregarding the proprietorship of the Lord. Disobeying the laws of nature or the order of the Lord brings ruin to a human being. Conversely, one who is sober, who knows the laws of nature, and who is not influenced by unnecessary attachment or aversion is sure to be recognized by the Lord and thus become eligible to go back to Godhead, back to the eternal home.

Mantra Two

कुर्वन्नेवेह कर्माणि जिजीविषेच्छतꣳ समाः ।
एवं त्वयि नान्यथेतोऽस्ति न कर्म लिप्यते नरे ॥ २ ॥

kurvann eveha karmāṇi
jijīviṣec chataṁ samāḥ
evaṁ tvayi nānyatheto 'sti
na karma lipyate nare

kurvan—doing continuously; *eva*—thus; *iha*—during this span of life; *karmāṇi*—work; *jijīviṣet*—one should desire to live; *śatam*—one hundred; *samāḥ*—years; *evam*—so living; *tvayi*—unto you; *na*—no; *anyathā*—alternative; *itaḥ*—from this path; *asti*—there is; *na*—not; *karma*—work; *lipyate*—can be bound; *nare*—unto a man.

TRANSLATION

One may aspire to live for hundreds of years if he continuously goes on working in that way, for that sort of work will not bind him to the law of karma. There is no alternative to this way for man.

PURPORT

No one wants to die: everyone wants to live as long as he can drag on. This tendency is visible not only individually but also collectively in the community, society and nation. There is a hard struggle for life by all kinds of living entities, and the *Vedas* say that this is quite natural. The living being is eternal by nature, but due to his bondage in material existence he has to change his body over and over. This process is called transmigration of the soul or *karma-bandhana*, bondage by one's work. The living entity has to work for his livelihood because that is the law of material nature, and if he does not act according to his prescribed duties, he transgresses the law of nature and binds himself more and more to the cycle of birth and death in the many species of life.

Other life forms are also subject to the cycle of birth and death, but when the living entity attains a human life, he gets a chance to get free from the chains of *karma*. *Karma, akarma* and *vikarma* are very clearly described in the *Bhagavad-gītā*. Actions that are performed in terms of one's prescribed duties, as mentioned in the revealed scriptures, are called *karma*. Actions that free one from the cycle of birth and death are called *akarma*. And actions that are performed through the misuse of one's freedom and that direct one to the lower life forms are called *vikarma*. Of these three types of action, that which frees one from the bondage to *karma* is preferred by intelligent men. Ordinary men wish to perform good work in order to be recognized and achieve some higher status of life in this world or in heaven, but more advanced men want to be free altogether from the actions and reactions of work. Intelligent men well know that both good and bad work equally bind one to the material miseries. Consequently they seek that work which will free them from the reactions of both good and bad work. Such liberating work is described here in the pages of *Śrī Īśopaniṣad.*

The instructions of *Śrī Īśopaniṣad* are more elaborately explained in the *Bhagavad-gītā,* sometimes called the *Gītopaniṣad,* the cream of all the *Upaniṣads.* In the *Bhagavad-gītā* (3.9–16) the Personality of Godhead says that one cannot attain the state of *naiṣkarmya,* or *akarma,* without executing the prescribed duties mentioned in the Vedic literature. This literature can regulate the working energy of a human being in such a way that he can gradually realize the authority of the Supreme Being. When he realizes the authority of the Personality of Godhead—Vāsudeva, or Kṛṣṇa—it is to be understood that he has attained the stage of positive knowledge. In this purified stage the modes of nature—namely goodness, passion and ignorance—cannot act, and he is able to work on the basis of *naiṣkarmya.* Such work does not bind one to the cycle of birth and death.

Factually, no one has to do anything more than render devotional service to the Lord. However, in the lower stages of life one cannot immediately adopt the activities of devotional service, nor can one completely stop fruitive work. A conditioned soul is accustomed to working for sense gratification—for his own selfish interest, immediate or extended. An ordinary man works for his own sense enjoyment, and when this principle of sense enjoyment is extended to include his society, nation or humanity in general, it assumes various attractive names such as altruism, socialism, communism, nationalism and humanitarianism. These "isms" are certainly very attractive forms of *karma-bandhana* (karmic bondage), but the Vedic instruction of *Śrī Īśopaniṣad* is that if one actually wants to live for any of the above "isms," he should make them God-centered. There is no harm in becoming a family man, or an altruist, a socialist, a communist, a nationalist or a humanitarian, provided that one executes his activities in relation with *īśāvāsya,* the God-centered conception.

In the *Bhagavad-gītā* (2.40) Lord Kṛṣṇa states that God-centered activities are so valuable that just a few of them can save a person from the greatest danger. The greatest danger of life is the danger of gliding down again into the evolutionary cycle of birth and death among the 8,400,000 species. If somehow or other a man misses the spiritual opportunity afforded by his human form of life and falls down again into the evolutionary cycle, he must be considered most unfortunate. Due to his defective senses, a foolish man cannot see that this is happening. Consequently *Śrī Īśopaniṣad* advises us to exert our energy in the spirit of *īśāvāsya.* Being so engaged, we may wish to live for many, many years; otherwise a long life in itself has no value. A tree lives for hundreds and hundreds of years, but there is no point in living a long time like trees, or breathing like bellows, or begetting children like hogs and dogs, or eating like camels. A humble God-centered life is more valuable than a colossal hoax of a life dedicated to godless altruism or socialism.

When altruistic activities are executed in the spirit of *Śrī Īśopaniṣad,* they become a form of *karma-yoga.* Such activities are recommended in the *Bhagavad-gītā* (18.5–9), for they guarantee their executor protection from the danger of sliding down into the evolutionary process of birth and death. Even though such God-centered activities may be half-finished, they are still good for the executor because they will guarantee him a human form in his next birth. In this way one can have another chance to improve his position on the path of liberation.

How one can execute God-centered activities is elaborately explained in the *Bhakti-rasāmṛta-sindhu,* by Śrīla Rūpa Gosvāmī. We have rendered this book into English as *The Nectar of Devotion.* We recommend this valuable book to all who are interested in performing their activities in the spirit of *Śrī Īśopaniṣad.*

Mantra Three

असुर्या नाम ते लोका अन्धेन तमसावृताः ।
तांस्ते प्रेत्याभिगच्छन्ति ये के चात्महनो जनाः ॥ ३ ॥

asuryā nāma te lokā
andhena tamasāvṛtāḥ
tām̐s te pretyābhigacchanti
ye ke cātma-hano janāḥ

asuryāḥ—meant for the *asuras; nāma*—famous by the name; *te*—those; *lokāḥ*—planets; *andhena*—by ignorance; *tamasā*—by darkness; *āvṛtāḥ*—covered; *tān*—those planets; *te*—they; *pretya*—after death; *abhigacchanti*—enter into; *ye*—anyone; *ke*—everyone; *ca*—and; *ātma-hanaḥ*—the killers of the soul; *janāḥ*—persons.

TRANSLATION

The killer of the soul, whoever he may be, must enter into the planets known as the worlds of the faithless, full of darkness and ignorance.

PURPORT

Human life is distinguished from animal life due to its heavy responsibilities. Those who are cognizant of these responsibilities and who work in that spirit are called *suras* (godly persons), and those who are neglectful of these responsibilities or who have no information of them are called *asuras* (demons). Throughout the universe there are only these two types of human being. In the *Ṛg Veda* it is stated that the *suras* always aim at the lotus feet of the Supreme Lord Viṣṇu and act accordingly. Their ways are as illuminated as the path of the sun.

Intelligent human beings must always remember that the soul obtains a human form after an evolution of many millions of years in the cycle of transmigration. The material world is sometimes compared to an ocean, and the human body is compared to a solid boat designed especially to cross this ocean. The Vedic scriptures and the *ācāryas,* or saintly teachers, are compared to expert boatmen, and the facilities of the human body are compared to favorable breezes that help the boat ply smoothly to its desired destination. If, with all these facilities, a human being does not fully utilize his life for self-realization, he must be considered *ātma-hā,* a killer of the soul. *Śrī Īśopaniṣad* warns in clear terms that the killer of the soul is destined to enter into the darkest region of ignorance to suffer perpetually.

There are swine, dogs, camels, asses, etc., whose economic necessities are just as important to them as ours are to us, but the economic problems of these animals are solved only under nasty and unpleasant conditions. The human being is given all facilities for a comfortable life by the laws of nature because the human form of life is more important and valuable than animal life. Why is man given a better life than that of the swine and other animals? Why is a highly placed government servant given better facilities than those of an ordinary clerk? The answer is that a highly placed officer has to discharge duties of a higher nature. Similarly, the duties human beings have to perform are higher than those of animals, who are always engaged in simply feeding their hungry stomachs. Yet the modern soul-killing civilization has only increased the problems of the hungry stomach. When we approach a polished animal in the form of a modern civilized man and ask him to take interest in self-realization, he will say that he simply wants to work to satisfy his stomach and that there is no need of self-realization for a hungry man. The laws of nature are so cruel, however, that despite his denunciation of the need for self-realization and his eagerness to work hard to fill his stomach, he is always threatened by unemployment.

We are given this human form of life not to work hard like asses, swine and dogs but to attain the highest perfection of life. If we do not care for self-realization, the laws of nature force us to work very hard, even though we may not want to do so. Human beings in this age have been forced to work hard like the asses and bullocks that pull carts. Some of the regions where the *asuras* are sent to work are revealed in this verse of *Śrī Īśopaniṣad.* If a man fails to discharge his duties as a human being, he is forced to transmigrate to the *asurya* planets and take birth in degraded species of life to work hard in ignorance and darkness.

In the *Bhagavad-gītā* (6.41–43) it is stated that a man who enters upon the path of self-realization but does not complete the process, despite having sincerely tried to realize his relationship with God, is given a chance to appear in a family of *śuci* or *śrīmat.* The word *śuci* indicates a spiritually advanced *brāhmaṇa,* and *śrīmat* indicates a *vaiśya,* a member of the mercantile community. So the person who fails to achieve self-realization is given a better chance in his next life, due to his sincere efforts in this life. If even a fallen candidate is given a chance to take birth in a respectable and noble family, one can hardly imagine the status of one who has achieved success. By simply attempting to realize God, one is guaranteed birth in a wealthy or aristocratic family. But those who do not even make an attempt, who want to be covered by illusion, who are too materialistic and too attached to material enjoyment, must enter into the darkest regions of hell, as confirmed throughout the Vedic literature. Such materialistic *asuras* sometimes make a show of religion, but their ultimate aim is material prosperity. The *Bhagavad-gītā* (16.17–18) rebukes such men by calling them *ātma-sambhāvita,* meaning that they are considered great only on the strength of deception and are empowered by the votes of the ignorant and by their own material wealth. Such *asuras,* devoid of self-realization and knowledge of *īśāvāsya,* the Lord's universal proprietorship, are certain to enter into the darkest regions.

The conclusion is that as human beings we are meant not simply for solving economic problems on a tottering platform but for solving all the problems of the material life into which we have been placed by the laws of nature.

Mantra Four

अनेजदेकं मनसो जवीयो नैनद्देवा आप्नुवन् पूर्वमर्षत् ।
तद्धावतोऽन्यानत्येति तिष्ठत्तस्मिन्नपो मातरिश्वा दधाति ॥ ४ ॥

anejad ekaṁ manaso javīyo
nainad devā āpnuvan pūrvam arṣat
tad dhāvato 'nyān atyeti tiṣṭhat
tasminn apo mātariśvā dadhāti

anejat—fixed; *ekam*—one; *manasaḥ*—than the mind; *javīyaḥ*—more swift; *na*—not; *enat*—this Supreme Lord; *devāḥ*—the demigods like Indra, etc.; *āpnuvan*—can approach; *pūrvam*—in front; *arṣat*—moving quickly; *tat*—He; *dhāvataḥ*—those who are running; *anyān*—others; *atyeti*—surpasses; *tiṣṭhat*—remaining in one place; *tasmin*—in Him; *apaḥ*—rain; *mātariśvā*—the gods who control the wind and rain; *dadhāti*—supply.

TRANSLATION

Although fixed in His abode, the Personality of Godhead is swifter than the mind and can overcome all others running. The powerful demigods cannot approach Him. Although in one place, He controls those who supply the air and rain. He surpasses all in excellence.

PURPORT

Through mental speculation, even the greatest philosopher cannot know the Supreme Lord, who is the Absolute Personality of Godhead. He can be known only by His devotees through His mercy. In the *Brahma-saṁhitā* (5.34) it is stated that even if a nondevotee philosopher travels through space at the speed of the wind or the mind for hundreds of millions of years, he will still find that the Absolute Truth is far, far away from him. The *Brahma-saṁhitā* (5.37) further describes that the Absolute Personality of Godhead has His transcendental abode, known as Goloka, where He remains and engages in His pastimes, yet by His inconceivable potencies He can simultaneously reach every part of His creative energy. In the *Viṣṇu Purāṇa* His potencies are compared to the heat and light that emanate from a fire. Although situated in one place, a fire can distribute its light and heat for some distance; similarly, the Absolute Personality of Godhead, although fixed in His transcendental abode, can diffuse His different energies everywhere.

Although His energies are innumerable, they can be divided into three principal categories: the internal potency, the marginal potency and the external potency. There are hundreds and millions of subheadings to each of these categories. The dominating demigods who are empowered to control and administer such natural phenomena as air, light and rain are all classified within the marginal potency of the Absolute Person. Lesser living beings, including humans, also belong to the Lord's marginal potency. The material world is the creation of the Lord's external potency. And the spiritual sky, where the kingdom of God is situated, is the manifestation of His internal potency.

Thus the different energies of the Lord are present everywhere. Although the Lord and His energies are nondifferent, one should not mistake these energies for the Supreme Truth. Nor should one wrongly consider that the Supreme Lord is distributed everywhere impersonally or that He loses His personal existence. Men are accustomed to reach conclusions according to their capacity for understanding, but the Supreme Lord is not subject to our limited capacity for understanding. It is for this reason that the *Upaniṣads* warn us that no one can approach the Lord by his own limited potency.

In the *Bhagavad-gītā* (10.2) the Lord says that not even the great *ṛṣis* and *suras* can know Him. And what to speak of the *asuras,* for whom there is no question of understanding the ways of the Lord? This fourth *mantra* of *Śrī Īśopaniṣad* very clearly suggests that the Absolute Truth is ultimately the Absolute Person; otherwise there would have been no need to mention so many details in support of His personal features.

Although the individual parts and parcels of the Lord's potencies have all the symptoms of the Lord Himself, they have limited spheres of activity and are therefore all limited. The parts and parcels are never equal to the whole; therefore they cannot appreciate the Lord's full potency. Under the influence of material nature, foolish and ignorant living beings who are but parts and parcels of the Lord try to conjecture about the Lord's transcendental position. *Śrī*

Īśopaniṣad warns of the futility of trying to establish the identity of the Lord through mental speculation. One should try to learn of the Transcendence from the Lord Himself, the supreme source of the *Vedas,* for the Lord alone has full knowledge of the Transcendence.

Every part and parcel of the Complete Whole is endowed with some particular energy to act according to the Lord's will. When the part-and-parcel living entity forgets his particular activities under the Lord's will, he is considered to be in *māyā,* illusion. Thus from the very beginning *Śrī Īśopaniṣad* warns us to be very careful to play the part designated for us by the Lord. This does not mean that the individual soul has no initiative of his own. Because he is part and parcel of the Lord, he must partake of the initiative of the Lord as well. When a person properly utilizes his initiative, or active nature, with intelligence, understanding that everything is the Lord's potency, he can revive his original consciousness, which was lost due to association with *māyā,* the external energy.

All power is obtained from the Lord; therefore each particular power must be utilized to execute the will of the Lord and not otherwise. The Lord can be known by one who has adopted such a submissive service attitude. Perfect knowledge means knowing the Lord in all His features, knowing His potencies and knowing how these potencies work by His will. These matters are described by the Lord in the *Bhagavad-gītā,* the essence of all the *Upaniṣads.*

Mantra Five

तदेजति तन्नैजति तद् दूरे तद्वन्तिके ।
तदन्तरस्य सर्वस्य तदु सर्वस्यास्य बाह्यतः ॥ ५ ॥

tad ejati tan naijati
tad dūre tad v antike
tad antar asya sarvasya
tad u sarvasyāsya bāhyataḥ

tat—this Supreme Lord; *ejati*—walks; *tat*—He; *na*—not; *ejati*—walks; *tat*—He; *dūre*—far away; *tat*—He; *u*—also; *antike*—very near; *tat*—He; *antaḥ*—within; *asya*—of this; *sarvasya*—of all; *tat*—He; *u*—also; *sarvasya*—of all; *asya*—of this; *bāhyataḥ*—external to.

TRANSLATION

The Supreme Lord walks and does not walk. He is far away, but He is very near as well. He is within everything, and yet He is outside of everything.

PURPORT

Here is a description of some of the Supreme Lord's transcendental activities, executed by His inconceivable potencies. The contradictions given here prove the inconceivable potencies of the Lord. "He walks, and He does not walk." Ordinarily, if someone can walk, it is illogical to say he cannot walk. But in reference to God, such a contradiction simply serves to indicate His inconceivable power. With our limited fund of knowledge we cannot accommodate such contradictions, and therefore we conceive of the Lord in terms of our limited powers of understanding. For example, the impersonalist philosophers of the Māyāvāda school accept only the Lord's impersonal activities and reject His personal feature. But the members of the Bhāgavata school, adopting the perfect conception of the Lord, accept His inconceivable potencies and thus understand that He is both personal and impersonal. The *bhāgavatas* know that without inconceivable potencies there can be no meaning to the words "Supreme Lord."

We should not take it for granted that because we cannot see God with our eyes the Lord has no personal existence. *Śrī Īśopaniṣad* refutes this argument by declaring that the Lord is far away but very near also. The abode of the Lord is beyond the material sky, and we have no means to measure even this material sky. If the material sky extends so far, then what to speak of the spiritual sky, which is altogether beyond it? That the spiritual sky is situated far, far away from the material universe is confirmed in the *Bhagavad-gītā* (15.6). But despite the Lord's being so far away, He can at once, within less than a second, descend before us with a speed swifter than that of the mind or wind. He can also run so swiftly that no one can surpass Him. This has already been described in the previous verse.

Yet when the Personality of Godhead comes before us, we neglect Him. Such foolish negligence is condemned by the Lord in the *Bhagavad-gītā* (9.11), where He says that the foolish deride Him, considering Him a mortal being. He is not a mortal being, nor does He come before us with a body produced of material nature. There are many so-called scholars who contend that the Lord descends in a body made of matter, just like an ordinary living being. Not knowing His inconceivable power, such foolish men place the Lord on an equal level with ordinary men.

Because He is full of inconceivable potencies, God can accept our service through any sort of medium, and He can convert His different potencies according to His own will. Nonbelievers argue either that the Lord cannot incarnate Himself at all, or that if He does He descends in a form of material energy. These arguments are nullified if we accept the existence of the Lord's inconceivable potencies. Then we will understand that even if the Lord appears before us in the form of material energy, it is quite possible for Him to convert this energy into spiritual energy. Since the source of the energies is one and the same, the energies can be utilized according to the will of their source. For example, the Lord can appear in the form of the *arcā-vigraha,* a Deity supposedly made of earth, stone or wood. Deity forms, although engraved from wood, stone or other matter, are not idols, as the iconoclasts contend.

In our present state of imperfect material existence, we cannot see the Supreme Lord due to imperfect vision. Yet those devotees who want to see Him by means of material vision are favored by the Lord, who appears in a so-called material form to accept His devotees' service. One should not think that such devotees, who are in the lowest stage of devotional service, are worshiping an idol. They are factually worshiping the Lord, who has agreed to appear before them in an approachable way. Nor is the *arcā* form fashioned according to the whims of the worshiper. This form is eternally existent with all paraphernalia. This can be actually felt by a sincere devotee, but not by an atheist.

In the *Bhagavad-gītā* (4.11) the Lord says that how He treats His devotee depends on the devotee's degree of surrender. The Lord reserves the right not to reveal Himself to anyone and everyone but to show Himself only to those souls who surrender unto Him. Thus for the surrendered soul He is always within reach, whereas for the unsurrendered soul He is far, far away and cannot be approached.

In this connection, two words the revealed scriptures often apply to the Lord—*saguṇa* ("with qualities") and *nirguṇa* ("without qualities")—are very important. The word *saguṇa* does not imply that when the Lord appears with perceivable qualities He must take on a material form and be subject to the laws of material nature. For Him there is no difference between the material and spiritual energies, because He is the source of all energies. As the controller of all energies, He cannot at any time be under their influence, as we are. The material energy works according to His direction; therefore He can use that energy for His purposes without ever being influenced by any of the qualities of that energy. (In this sense He is *nirguṇa,* "without qualities.") Nor does the Lord become a formless entity at any time, for ultimately He is the eternal form, the primeval

Lord. His impersonal aspect, or Brahman effulgence, is but the glow of His personal rays, just as the sun's rays are the glow of the sun-god.

When the child saint Prahlāda Mahārāja was in the presence of his atheist father, his father asked him, "Where is your God?" When Prahlāda replied that God resides everywhere, the father angrily asked whether his God was within one of the pillars of the palace, and the child said yes. At once the atheist king shattered the pillar in front of him to pieces, and the Lord instantly appeared as Nṛsiṁha, the half-man, half-lion incarnation, and killed the atheist king. Thus the Lord is within everything, and He creates everything by His different energies. Through His inconceivable powers He can appear at any place in order to favor His sincere devotee. Lord Nṛsiṁha appeared from within the pillar not by the order of the atheist king but by the wish of His devotee Prahlāda. An atheist cannot order the Lord to appear, but the Lord will appear anywhere and everywhere to show mercy to His devotee. The *Bhagavad-gītā* (4.8) similarly states that the Lord appears in order to vanquish nonbelievers and protect believers. Of course, the Lord has sufficient energies and agents who can vanquish atheists, but it pleases Him to personally favor a devotee. Therefore He descends as an incarnation. Actually, He descends only to favor His devotees and not for any other purpose.

In the *Brahma-saṁhitā* (5.35) it is said that Govinda, the primeval Lord, enters everything by His plenary portion. He enters the universe as well as all the atoms of the universe. He is outside in His *virāṭ* form, and He is within everything as *antaryāmī*. As *antaryāmī* He witnesses everything that is going on, and He awards us the results of our actions as *karma-phala*. We ourselves may forget what we have done in previous lives, but because the Lord witnesses our actions, the results of our actions are always there, and we have to undergo the reactions nonetheless.

The fact is that there is nothing but God within and without. Everything is a manifestation of His different energies, like the heat and light emanating from a fire, and in this way there is a oneness among His diverse energies. Although there is oneness, however, the Lord in His personal form still enjoys unlimitedly all the pleasures enjoyed minutely by the tiny part-and-parcel living entities.

Mantra Six

यस्तु सर्वाणि भूतान्यात्मन्येवानुपश्यति ।
सर्वभूतेषु चात्मानं ततो न विजुगुप्सते ॥ ६ ॥

yas tu sarvāṇi bhūtāny
ātmany evānupaśyati
sarva-bhūteṣu cātmānaṁ
tato na vijugupsate

yaḥ—he who; *tu*—but; *sarvāṇi*—all; *bhūtāni*—living entities; *ātmani*—in relation to the Supreme Lord; *eva*—only; *anupaśyati*—observes in a systematic way; *sarva-bhūteṣu*—in every living being; *ca*—and; *ātmānam*—the Supersoul; *tataḥ*—thereafter; *na*—not; *vijugupsate*—hates anyone.

TRANSLATION

He who sees everything in relation to the Supreme Lord, who sees all living entities as His parts and parcels, and who sees the Supreme Lord within everything never hates anything or any being.

PURPORT

This is a description of the *mahā-bhāgavata,* the great personality who sees everything in relation to the Supreme Personality of Godhead. The Supreme

Lord's presence is realized in three stages. The *kaniṣṭha-adhikārī* is in the lowest stage of realization. He goes to a place of worship, such as a temple, church or mosque, according to his religious faith, and worships there according to scriptural injunctions. Devotees in this stage consider the Lord to be present at the place of worship and nowhere else. They cannot ascertain who is in what position in devotional service, nor can they tell who has realized the Supreme Lord. Such devotees follow the routine formulas and sometimes quarrel among themselves, considering one type of devotion better than another. These *kaniṣṭha-adhikārīs* are actually materialistic devotees who are simply trying to transcend the material boundary to reach the spiritual plane.

Those who have attained the second stage of realization are called *madhyama-adhikārīs.* These devotees observe the distinctions between four categories of being: (1) the Supreme Lord; (2) the devotees of the Lord; (3) the innocent, who have no knowledge of the Lord; and (4) the atheists, who have no faith in the Lord and hate those in devotional service. The *madhyama-adhikārī* behaves differently toward these four classes of person. He adores the Lord, considering Him the object of love; he makes friends with those who are in devotional service; he tries to awaken the dormant love of God in the hearts of the innocent; and he avoids the atheists, who deride the very name of the Lord.

Above the *madhyama-adhikārī* is the *uttama-adhikārī,* who sees everything in relation to the Supreme Lord. Such a devotee does not discriminate between an atheist and a theist but sees everyone as part and parcel of God. He knows that there is no essential difference between a vastly learned *brāhmaṇa* and a dog in the street, because both of them are part and parcel of the Lord, although they are encaged in different bodies on account of the different qualities of their activities in their previous lives. He sees that the *brāhmaṇa* particle of the Supreme Lord has not misused his little independence given him by the Lord and that the dog particle has misused his independence and is therefore being punished by the laws of nature by being encaged in the form of a dog. Not considering the respective actions of the *brāhmaṇa* and the dog, the *uttama-adhikārī* tries to do good to both. Such a learned devotee is not misled by material bodies but is attracted by the spiritual spark within them.

Those who imitate an *uttama-adhikārī* by flaunting a sense of oneness or fellowship but who behave on the bodily platform are actually false philanthropists. The conception of universal brotherhood must be learned from an *uttama-adhikārī* and not from a foolish person who does not properly understand the individual soul or the Supreme Lord's Supersoul expansion, who dwells everywhere.

It is clearly mentioned in this sixth *mantra* that one should "observe," or systematically see. This means that one must follow the previous *ācārya,* the perfected teacher. *Anupaśyati* is the exact Sanskrit word used in this connection. *Anu* means "to follow," and *paśyati* means "to observe." Thus the word *anupaśyati* means that one should not see things as he does with the naked eye but should follow the previous *ācāryas*. Due to material defects, the naked eye cannot see anything properly. One cannot see properly unless one has heard from a superior source, and the highest source is the Vedic wisdom, which is spoken by the Lord Himself. Vedic truths are coming in disciplic succession from the Lord to Brahmā, from Brahmā to Nārada, from Nārada to Vyāsa, and from Vyāsa to many of his disciples. Formerly there was no need to record the messages of the *Vedas,* because people in earlier ages were more intelligent and had sharper memories. They could follow the instructions simply by hearing once from the mouth of a bona fide spiritual master.

At present there are many commentaries on the revealed scriptures, but most of them are not in the line of disciplic succession coming from Śrīla Vyāsadeva, who originally compiled the Vedic wisdom. The final, most perfect and sublime work by Śrīla Vyāsadeva is *Śrīmad-Bhāgavatam,* which is the natural commentary on the *Vedānta-sūtra.* There is also the *Bhagavad-gītā,* which was spoken by the Lord Himself and recorded by Vyāsadeva. These are the most important revealed scriptures, and any commentary that contradicts the principles of the *Bhagavad-gītā* or *Śrīmad-Bhāgavatam* is unauthorized. There is complete agreement among the *Upaniṣads, Vedānta-sūtra, Vedas, Bhagavad-gītā* and *Śrīmad-Bhāgavatam,* and no one should try to reach any conclusion about the *Vedas* without receiving instructions from members of Vyāsadeva's disciplic succession, who believe in the Personality of Godhead and His diverse energies as they are explained in *Śrī Īśopaniṣad.*

According to the *Bhagavad-gītā* (18.54), only one

who is already on the liberated platform (*brahma-bhūta*) can become an *uttama-adhikārī* devotee and see every living being as his own brother. This vision cannot be had by politicians, who are always after some material gain. One who imitates the symptoms of an *uttama-adhikārī* may serve another's outward body for the purpose of fame or material reward, but he does not serve the spirit soul. Such an imitator can have no information of the spiritual world. The *uttama-adhikārī* sees the spirit soul within the material body and serves him as spirit. Thus the material aspect is automatically served.

Mantra Seven

यस्मिन् सर्वाणि भूतान्यात्मैवाभूद् विजानतः ।
तत्र को मोहः कः शोक एकत्वमनुपश्यतः ॥ ७ ॥

yasmin sarvāṇi bhūtāny
ātmaivābhūd vijānataḥ
tatra ko mohaḥ kaḥ śoka
ekatvam anupaśyataḥ

yasmin—in the situation; *sarvāṇi*—all; *bhūtāni*—living entities; *ātmā*—the *cit-kaṇa,* or spiritual spark; *eva*—only; *abhūt*—exist as; *vijānataḥ*—of one who knows; *tatra*—therein; *kaḥ*—what; *mohaḥ*—illusion; *kaḥ*—what; *śokaḥ*—anxiety; *ekatvam*—oneness in quality; *anupaśyataḥ*—of one who sees through authority, or one who sees constantly like that.

TRANSLATION

One who always sees all living entities as spiritual sparks, in quality one with the Lord, becomes a true knower of things. What, then, can be illusion or anxiety for him?

PURPORT

Except for the *madhyama-adhikārī* and *uttama-adhikārī* discussed above, no one can correctly see the spiritual position of a living being. The living entities are qualitatively one with the Supreme Lord, just as the sparks of a fire are qualitatively one with the fire. Yet sparks are not fire as far as quantity is concerned, for the quantity of heat and light present in the sparks is not equal to that in fire. The *mahā-bhāgavata,* the great devotee, sees oneness in the sense that he sees everything as the energy of the Supreme Lord. Since there is no difference between the energy and the energetic, there is the sense of oneness. Although from the analytical point of view heat and light are different from fire, there is no meaning to the word "fire" without heat and light. In synthesis, therefore, heat, light and fire are the same.

In this *mantra* the words *ekatvam anupaśyataḥ* indicate that one should see the unity of all living entities from the viewpoint of the revealed scriptures. The individual sparks of the supreme whole (the Lord) possess almost eighty percent of the known qualities of the whole, but they are not quantitatively equal to the Supreme Lord. These qualities are present in minute quantity, for the living entity is but a minute part and parcel of the supreme whole. To use another analogy, the quantity of salt present in a drop is never comparable to the quantity of salt present in the complete ocean, but the salt present in the drop is qualitatively equal in chemical composition to all the salt present in the ocean. If the individual living being were equal to the Supreme Lord both qualitatively and quantitatively, there would be no question of his being under the influence of the material energy. In the previous *mantras* it has already been discussed that no living being—not even the powerful demigods—can surpass the Supreme Being in any respect. Therefore *ekatvam* does not mean that a living being is equal in all respects to the Supreme Lord. It does, however, indicate that in a broader sense there is one interest, just as in a family the interest of all members is one, or in a nation the national interest is one, although there are many different individual citizens. Since the living entities are all members of the same supreme family, their interest and that of the Supreme Being are not different. Every living being is the son of the Supreme Being. As stated in the *Bhagavad-gītā* (7.5), all living creatures throughout the universe—including birds, reptiles, ants, aquatics, trees and so on—are emanations of the marginal potency of the Supreme Lord. Therefore all of them belong to the family of the Supreme Being. There is no clash of interest.

The spiritual entities are meant for enjoyment, as stated in the *Vedānta-sūtra* (1.1.12): *ānanda-mayo 'bhyāsāt.* By nature and constitution, every living being—including the Supreme Lord and each of His parts and parcels—is meant for eternal enjoyment. The living beings who are encaged in the material tabernacle are constantly seeking enjoyment, but they are seeking it on the wrong platform. Apart from the material platform is the spiritual platform, where the Supreme Being enjoys Himself with His innumerable associates. On that platform there is no trace of material qualities, and therefore that platform is called *nirguṇa.* On the *nirguṇa* platform there is never a clash over the object of enjoyment. Here in the material world there is always a clash between different individual beings because here the proper center of enjoyment is missed. The real center of enjoyment is the Supreme Lord, who is the center of the sublime and spiritual *rāsa* dance. We are all meant to join Him and enjoy life with one transcendental interest and without any clash. That is the highest platform of spiritual interest, and as soon as one realizes this perfect form of oneness, there can be no question of illusion (*moha*) or lamentation (*śoka*).

A godless civilization arises from illusion, and the result of such a civilization is lamentation. A godless civilization, such as that sponsored by the modern politicians, is always full of anxieties because it may be crushed at any moment. That is the law of nature. As stated in the *Bhagavad-gītā* (7.14), no one but those who surrender at the lotus feet of the Supreme Lord can surpass the stringent laws of nature. Thus if we wish to get rid of all sorts of illusion and anxiety and create unity out of all diverse interests, we must bring God into all our activities.

The results of our activities must be used to serve the interest of the Lord, and not for any other purpose. Only by serving the Lord's interest can we perceive the *ātma-bhūta* interest mentioned herein. The *ātma-bhūta* interest mentioned in this *mantra* and the *brahma-bhūta* interest mentioned in the *Bhagavad-gītā* (18.54) are one and the same. The supreme *ātmā,* or soul, is the Lord Himself, and the minute *ātmā* is the living entity. The supreme *ātmā,* or Paramātmā, alone maintains all the individual minute beings, for the Supreme Lord wants to derive pleasure out of their affection. The father extends himself through his children and maintains them in order to derive pleasure. If the children obey the father's will, family affairs will run smoothly, with one interest and a pleasing atmosphere. The same situation is transcendentally arranged in the absolute family of the Parabrahman, the Supreme Spirit.

The Parabrahman is as much a person as the individual entities. Neither the Lord nor the living entities are impersonal. Such transcendental personalities are full of transcendental bliss, knowledge and life eternal. That is the real position of spiritual existence, and as soon as one is fully cognizant of this transcendental position, he at once surrenders unto the lotus feet of the Supreme Being, Śrī Kṛṣṇa. But such a *mahātmā,* or great soul, is very rarely seen because such transcendental realization is achieved only after many, many births. Once it is attained, however, there is no longer any illusion or lamentation or the miseries of material existence or birth and death, which are all experienced in our present life. That is the information we get from this *mantra* of *Śrī Īśopaniṣad.*

Mantra Eight

स पर्यगाच्छुक्रमकायमव्रण-
    मस्नाविरꣳ शुद्धमपापविद्धम् ।
कविर्मनीषी परिभूः स्वयम्भूर्
    याथातथ्यतोऽर्थान् व्यदधाच्छाश्वतीभ्यः समाभ्यः ॥ ८ ॥

sa paryagāc chukram akāyam avraṇam
asnāviraṁ śuddham apāpa-viddham
kavir manīṣī paribhūḥ svayambhūr
yāthātathyato 'rthān vyadadhāc chāśvatībhyaḥ samābhyaḥ

saḥ—that person; *paryagāt*—must know in fact; *śukram*—the omnipotent; *akāyam*—unembodied; *avraṇam*—without reproach; *asnāviram*—without veins; *śuddham*—antiseptic; *apāpa-viddham*—prophylactic; *kaviḥ*—omniscient; *manīṣī*—philosopher; *paribhūḥ*—the greatest of all; *svayambhūḥ*—self-sufficient; *yāthātathyataḥ*—just in pursuance of; *arthān*—desirables; *vyadadhāt*—awards; *śāśvatībhyaḥ*—immemorial; *samābhyaḥ*—time.

TRANSLATION

Such a person must factually know the greatest of all, the Personality of Godhead, who is unembodied, omniscient, beyond reproach, without veins, pure

and uncontaminated, the self-sufficient philosopher who has been fulfilling everyone's desire since time immemorial.

PURPORT

Here is a description of the transcendental and eternal form of the Absolute Personality of Godhead. The Supreme Lord is not formless. He has His own transcendental form, which is not at all similar to the forms of the mundane world. The forms of the living entities in this world are embodied in material nature, and they work like any material machine. The anatomy of a material body must have a mechanical construction with veins and so forth, but the transcendental body of the Supreme Lord has nothing like veins. It is clearly stated here that He is unembodied, which means that there is no difference between His body and His soul. Nor is He forced to accept a body according to the laws of nature, as we are. In materially conditioned life, the soul is different from the gross embodiment and subtle mind. For the Supreme Lord, however, there is never any such difference between Him and His body and mind. He is the Complete Whole, and His mind, body and He Himself are all one and the same.

In the *Brahma-saṁhitā* (5.1) there is a similar description of the Supreme Lord. He is described there as *sac-cid-ānanda-vigraha,* which means that He is the eternal form fully representing transcendental existence, knowledge and bliss. As such, He does not require a separate body or mind, as we do in material existence. The Vedic literature clearly states that the Lord's transcendental body is completely different from ours; thus He is sometimes described as formless. This means that He has no form like ours and that He is devoid of a form we can conceive of. In the *Brahma-saṁhitā* (5.32) it is further stated that with each and every part of His body He can do the work of the other senses. This means that the Lord can walk with His hands, accept things with His legs, see with His hands and feet, eat with His eyes, etc. In the *śruti-mantras* it is also said that although the Lord has no hands and legs like ours, He has a different type of hands and legs, by which He can accept all that we offer Him and run faster than anyone. These points are confirmed in this eighth *mantra* through the use of words like *śukram* ("omnipotent").

The Lord's worshipable form (*arcā-vigraha*), which is installed in temples by authorized *ācāryas* who have realized the Lord in terms of Mantra Seven, is nondifferent from the original form of the Lord. The Lord's original form is that of Śrī Kṛṣṇa, and Śrī Kṛṣṇa expands Himself into an unlimited number of forms, such as Baladeva, Rāma, Nṛsiṁha and Varāha. All of these forms are one and the same Personality of Godhead. Similarly, the *arcā-vigraha* worshiped in temples is also an expanded form of the Lord. By worshiping the *arcā-vigraha,* one can at once approach the Lord, who accepts the service of a devotee by His omnipotent energy. The *arcā-vigraha* of the Lord descends at the request of the *ācāryas,* the holy teachers, and works exactly in the original way of the Lord by virtue of the Lord's omnipotence. Foolish people who have no knowledge of *Śrī Īśopaniṣad* or of any of the other *śruti-mantras* consider the *arcā-vigraha,* which is worshiped by pure devotees, to be made of material elements. This form may be seen as material by the imperfect eyes of foolish people or *kaniṣṭha-adhikārīs,* but such people do not know that the Lord, being omnipotent and omniscient, can transform matter into spirit and spirit into matter, as He desires.

In the *Bhagavad-gītā* (9.11–12) the Lord regrets the fallen condition of men with little knowledge who deride Him because He descends like a man into this world. Such poorly informed persons do not know the omnipotence of the Lord. Thus the Lord does not manifest Himself in full to the mental speculators. He can be appreciated only in proportion to one's surrender to Him. The fallen condition of the living entities is due entirely to forgetfulness of their relationship with God.

In this *mantra,* as well as in many other Vedic *mantras,* it is clearly stated that the Lord has been supplying goods to the living entities from time immemorial. A living being desires something, and the Lord supplies the object of that desire in proportion to one's qualification. If a man wants to be a high-court judge, he must acquire not only the necessary qualifications but also the consent of the authority who can award the title of high-court judge. The qualifications in themselves are insufficient for one to occupy the post: it must be awarded by some superior authority. Similarly, the Lord awards enjoyment to living entities in proportion to their qualifications, but good qualifications in themselves are not sufficient to enable one to receive awards. The mercy of the Lord is also required.

Ordinarily the living being does not know what to

be made of material elements. This form
n as material by the imperfect eyes of
ɔle or *kaniṣṭha-adhikārīs,* but such people
w that the Lord, being omnipotent and
can transform matter into spirit and spirit
as He desires.

hagavad-gītā (9.11–12) the Lord regrets
condition of men with little knowledge
Him because He descends like a man
rld. Such poorly informed persons do not
mnipotence of the Lord. Thus the Lord
nifest Himself in full to the mental specu-
an be appreciated only in proportion to
ıder to Him. The fallen condition of the
es is due entirely to forgetfulness of their
with God.

ıantra, as well as in many other Vedic
is clearly stated that the Lord has been
ɔods to the living entities from time im-
living being desires something, and the
es the object of that desire in proportion
ılification. If a man wants to be a high-
he must acquire not only the necessary
ıs but also the consent of the authority
vard the title of high-court judge. The
ıs in themselves are insufficient for one
he post: it must be awarded by some
hority. Similarly, the Lord awards enjoy-
ıg entities in proportion to their qualifi-
good qualifications in themselves are not
enable one to receive awards. The mercy
is also required.

y the living being does not know what to

Mantra Eight

स पर्यगाच्छुक्रमकायमव्रण-
मस्नाविरꣳ शुद्धमपापविद्धम् ।
कविर्मनीषी परिभूः स्वयम्भूर्
याथातथ्यतोऽर्थान् व्यदधाच्छाश्वतीभ्यः समाभ्यः ॥ ८ ॥

sa paryagāc chukram akāyam avraṇam
asnāviraṁ śuddham apāpa-viddham
kavir manīṣī paribhūḥ svayambhūr
yāthātathyato 'rthān vyadadhāc chāśvatībhyaḥ samābhyaḥ

saḥ—that person; *paryagāt*—must know in fact; *śukram*—the omnipotent; *akāyam*—unembodied; *avraṇam*—without reproach; *asnāviram*—without veins; *śuddham*—antiseptic; *apāpa-viddham*—prophylactic; *kaviḥ*—omniscient; *manīṣī*—philosopher; *paribhūḥ*—the greatest of all; *svayambhūḥ*—self-sufficient; *yāthātathyataḥ*—just in pursuance of; *arthān*—desirables; *vyadadhāt*—awards; *śāśvatībhyaḥ*—immemorial; *samābhyaḥ*—time.

TRANSLATION

Such a person must factually know the greatest of all, the Personality of Godhead, who is unembodied, omniscient, beyond reproach, without veins, pure

and uncontaminated, the self-sufficient philosopher who has been fulfilling everyone's desire since time immemorial.

PURPORT

Here is a description of the transcendental and eternal form of the Absolute Personality of Godhead. The Supreme Lord is not formless. He has His own transcendental form, which is not at all similar to the forms of the mundane world. The forms of the living entities in this world are embodied in material nature, and they work like any material machine. The anatomy of a material body must have a mechanical construction with veins and so forth, but the transcendental body of the Supreme Lord has nothing like veins. It is clearly stated here that He is unembodied, which means that there is no difference between His body and His soul. Nor is He forced to accept a body according to the laws of nature, as we are. In materially conditioned life, the soul is different from the gross embodiment and subtle mind. For the Supreme Lord, however, there is never any such difference between Him and His body and mind. He is the Complete Whole, and His mind, body and He Himself are all one and the same.

In the *Brahma-saṁhitā* (5.1) there is a similar description of the Supreme Lord. He is described there as *sac-cid-ānanda-vigraha,* which means that He is the eternal form fully representing transcendental existence, knowledge and bliss. As such, He does not require a separate body or mind, as we do in material existence. The Vedic literature clearly states that the Lord's transcendental body is completely

different from ours; thu
as formless. This means t
and that He is devoid of a
the *Brahma-saṁhitā* (5.3
with each and every part
work of the other senses.
can walk with His hands, a
see with His hands and fee
the *śruti-mantras* it is also sa
has no hands and legs like
type of hands and legs, by
that we offer Him and run fa
points are confirmed in this
the use of words like *śukram*

The Lord's worshipable for
is installed in temples by au
have realized the Lord in term
nondifferent from the original
Lord's original form is that
Kṛṣṇa expands Himself into a
forms, such as Baladeva, Rām
All of these forms are one an
of Godhead. Similarly, the *a*
in temples is also an expande
worshiping the *arcā-vigraha*
proach the Lord, who accep
tee by His omnipotent ene
the Lord descends at the re
holy teachers, and works e
of the Lord by virtue of
Foolish people who hav
Īśopaniṣad or of any of th
sider the *arcā-vigraha,* wh

devotees
may be
foolish
do not
omnisc
into m
In
the fa
who
into
know
does
lato
one
livi
rel
su
me
Lo
to
cou
qua
who
qua
to c
supe
men
catio
suffi
of th
O

ask from the Lord, nor which post to seek. When the living being comes to know his constitutional position, however, he asks to be accepted into the transcendental association of the Lord in order to render transcendental loving service unto Him. Unfortunately, living beings under the influence of material nature ask for many other things, and they are described in the *Bhagavad-gītā* (2.41) as having divided, or splayed, intelligence. Spiritual intelligence is one, but mundane intelligence is diverse. In *Śrīmad-Bhāgavatam* (7.5.30–31) it is stated that those who are captivated by the temporary beauties of the external energy forget the real aim of life, which is to go back to Godhead. Forgetting this, one tries to adjust things by various plans and programs, but this is like chewing what has already been chewed. Nonetheless, the Lord is so kind that He allows the forgetful living entity to continue in this way without interference. Thus this *mantra* of *Śrī Īśopaniṣad* uses the very appropriate word *yāthātathyataḥ,* indicating that the Lord rewards the living entities just in pursuance of their desires. If a living being wants to go to hell, the Lord allows him to do so without interference, and if he wants to go back home, back to Godhead, the Lord helps him.

God is described here as *paribhūḥ,* the greatest of all. No one is greater than or equal to Him. Other living beings are described here as beggars who ask goods from the Lord. The Lord supplies the things the living entities desire. If the entities were equal to the Lord in potency—if they were omnipotent and omniscient—there would be no question of their begging from the Lord, even for so-called liberation.

Real liberation means going back to Godhead. Liberation as conceived by an impersonalist is a myth, and begging for sense gratification has to continue eternally unless the beggar comes to his spiritual senses and realizes his constitutional position.

Only the Supreme Lord is self-sufficient. When Lord Kṛṣṇa appeared on earth five thousand years ago, He displayed His full manifestation as the Personality of Godhead through His various activities. In His childhood He killed many powerful demons, such as Aghāsura, Bakāsura and Śakaṭāsura, and there was no question of His having acquired such power through any extraneous endeavor. He lifted Govardhana Hill without ever practicing weightlifting. He danced with the *gopīs* without social restriction and without reproach. Although the *gopīs* approached Him with a paramour's feelings of love, the relationship between the *gopīs* and Lord Kṛṣṇa was worshiped even by Lord Caitanya, who was a strict *sannyāsī* and rigid follower of disciplinary regulations. To confirm that the Lord is always pure and uncontaminated, *Śrī Īśopaniṣad* describes Him as *śuddham* (antiseptic) and *apāpa-viddham* (prophylactic). He is antiseptic in the sense that even an impure thing can become purified just by touching Him. The word "prophylactic" refers to the power of His association. As mentioned in the *Bhagavad-gītā* (9.30–31), a devotee may appear to be *su-durācāra,* not well behaved, in the beginning, but he should be accepted as pure because he is on the right path. This is due to the prophylactic nature of the Lord's association. The Lord is also *apāpa-viddham* because sin cannot touch Him. Even if He acts in a way that appears to be sinful, such actions are all-good, for there is no question of His being affected by sin. Because in all circumstances He is *śuddham,* most purified, He is often compared to the sun. The sun extracts moisture from many untouchable places on the earth, yet it remains pure. In fact, it purifies obnoxious things by virtue of its sterilizing powers. If the sun, which is a material object, is so powerful, then we can hardly begin to imagine the purifying strength of the all-powerful Lord.

Mantra Nine

अन्धं तमः प्रविशन्ति येऽविद्यामुपासते ।
ततो भूय इव ते तमो य उ विद्यायाँ रताः ॥ ९ ॥

andhaṁ tamaḥ praviśanti
ye 'vidyām upāsate
tato bhūya iva te tamo
ya u vidyāyāṁ ratāḥ

andham—gross ignorance; *tamaḥ*—darkness; *praviśanti*—enter into; *ye*—those who; *avidyām*—nescience; *upāsate*—worship; *tataḥ*—than that; *bhūyaḥ*—still more; *iva*—like; *te*—they; *tamaḥ*—darkness; *ye*—those who; *u*—also; *vidyāyām*—in the culture of knowledge; *ratāḥ*—engaged.

TRANSLATION

Those who engage in the culture of nescient activities shall enter into the darkest region of ignorance. Worse still are those engaged in the culture of so-called knowledge.

PURPORT

This *mantra* offers a comparative study of *vidyā* and *avidyā*. *Avidyā,* or ignorance, is undoubtedly dangerous, but *vidyā,* or knowledge, is even more dangerous when mistaken or misguided. This *mantra* of *Śrī Īśopaniṣad* is more applicable today than at any time in the past. Modern civilization has advanced considerably in the field of mass education, but the result is that people are more unhappy than ever before because of the stress placed on material advancement to the exclusion of the most important part of life, the spiritual aspect.

As far as *vidyā* is concerned, the first *mantra* has explained very clearly that the Supreme Lord is the proprietor of everything and that forgetfulness of this fact is ignorance. The more a man forgets this fact of life, the more he is in darkness. In view of this, a godless civilization directed toward the so-called advancement of education is more dangerous than a civilization in which the masses of people are less "educated."

Of the different classes of men—*karmīs, jñānīs* and *yogīs*—the *karmīs* are those who are engaged in the activities of sense gratification. In the modern civilization, 99.9 percent of the people are engaged in the activities of sense gratification under the flags of industrialism, economic development, altruism, political activism, and so on. All these activities are more or less based on satisfaction of the senses, to the exclusion of the kind of God consciousness described in the first *mantra.*

In the language of the *Bhagavad-gītā* (7.15), people who are engaged in gross sense gratification are *mūḍhas*—asses. The ass is a symbol of stupidity. Those who simply engage in the profitless pursuit of sense gratification are worshiping *avidyā,* according to *Śrī Īśopaniṣad.* And those who play the role of helping this sort of civilization in the name of educational advancement are actually doing more harm than those who are on the platform of gross sense gratification. The advancement of learning by a godless people is as dangerous as a valuable jewel on the hood of a cobra. A cobra decorated with a valuable jewel is more dangerous than one not decorated. In the *Hari-bhakti-sudhodaya* (3.11.12), the advancement of education by a godless people is compared to decorations on a dead body. In India, as in many other countries, some people follow the custom of leading a procession with a decorated dead body for the pleasure of the lamenting relatives. In the same way, modern civilization is a patchwork of activities meant to cover the perpetual miseries of material existence. All such activities are aimed toward sense gratification. But above the senses is the mind, and above the mind is the intelligence, and above the intelligence is the soul. Thus the aim of real education should be self-realization, realization of the spiritual values of the soul. Any education which does not lead to such realization must be considered *avidyā,* or nescience. And to culture such nescience means to go down to the darkest region of ignorance.

According to the *Bhagavad-gītā* (2.42, 7.15), mistaken mundane educators are known as *veda-vāda-rata* and *māyayāpahṛta-jñāna.* They may also be atheistic demons, the lowest of men. Those who are *veda-vāda-rata* pose themselves as very learned in the Vedic literature, but unfortunately they are completely diverted from the purpose of the *Vedas.* In the *Bhagavad-gītā* (15.15) it is said that the purpose of the *Vedas* is to know the Personality of Godhead, but these *veda-vāda-rata* men are not at all interested in the Personality of Godhead. On the contrary, they are fascinated by such fruitive results as the attainment of heaven.

As stated in Mantra One, we should know that the Personality of Godhead is the proprietor of everything and that we must be satisfied with our allotted portions of the necessities of life. The purpose of all Vedic literature is to awaken this God consciousness in the forgetful living being, and this same purpose is presented in various ways in the different scriptures of the world for the understanding of a foolish mankind. Thus the ultimate purpose of all religions is to bring one back to Godhead.

But the *veda-vāda-rata* people, instead of realizing that the purpose of the *Vedas* is to revive the forgetful soul's lost relationship with the Personality of Godhead, take it for granted that such side issues as the attainment of heavenly pleasure for sense gratification—the lust for which causes their material bondage in the first place—are the ultimate end of the *Vedas*. Such people misguide others by misinterpreting the Vedic literature. Sometimes they even condemn the *Purāṇas,* which are authentic Vedic explanations for laymen. The *veda-vāda-ratas* give their own explanations of the *Vedas,* neglecting the authority of great teachers (*ācāryas*). They also tend to raise some unscrupulous person from among themselves and present him as the leading exponent of Vedic knowledge. Such *veda-vāda-ratas* are especially condemned in this *mantra* by the very appropriate Sanskrit words *vidyāyāṁ ratāḥ. Vidyāyām* refers to the study of the *Vedas* because the *Vedas* are the origin of all knowledge (*vidyā*), and *ratāḥ* means "those engaged." *Vidyāyāṁ ratāḥ* thus means "those engaged in the study of the *Vedas.*" The so-called students of the *Vedas* are condemned herein because they are ignorant of the actual purpose of the *Vedas* on account of their disobeying the *ācāryas.* Such *veda-vāda-ratas* search out meanings in every word of the *Vedas* to suit their own purposes. They do not know that the Vedic literature is a collection of extraordinary books that can be understood only through the chain of disciplic succession.

One must approach a bona fide spiritual master in order to understand the transcendental message of the *Vedas.* That is the direction of the *Muṇḍaka Upaniṣad* (1.2.12). These *veda-vāda-rata* people, however, have their own *ācāryas,* who are not in the chain of transcendental succession. Thus they progress into the darkest region of ignorance by misinterpreting the Vedic literature. They fall even further into ignorance than those who have no knowledge of the *Vedas* at all.

The *māyayāpahṛta-jñāna* class of men are self-made "Gods." Such men think that they themselves are God and that there is no need of worshiping any other God. They will agree to worship an ordinary man if he happens to be rich, but they will never worship the Personality of Godhead. Such men, unable to recognize their own foolishness, never consider how it is that God can be entrapped by *māyā,* His own illusory energy. If God were ever entrapped by *māyā, māyā* would be more powerful than God. Such men say that God is all-powerful, but they do not consider that if He is all-powerful there is no possibility of His being overpowered by *māyā.* These self-made "Gods" cannot answer all these questions very clearly; they are simply satisfied to have become "God" themselves.

Mantra Ten

अन्यदेवाहुर्विद्ययान्यदाहुरविद्यया ।
इति शुश्रुम धीराणां ये नस्तद् विचचक्षिरे ॥ १० ॥

anyad evāhur vidyayā-
nyad āhur avidyayā
iti śuśruma dhīrāṇāṁ
ye nas tad vicacakṣire

anyat—different; *eva*—certainly; *āhuḥ*—said; *vidyayā*—by culture of knowledge; *anyat*—different; *āhuḥ*—said; *avidyayā*—by culture of nescience; *iti*—thus; *śuśruma*—I heard; *dhīrāṇām*—from the sober; *ye*—who; *naḥ*—to us; *tat*—that; *vicacakṣire*—explained.

TRANSLATION

The wise have explained that one result is derived from the culture of knowledge and that a different result is obtained from the culture of nescience.

PURPORT

As advised in Chapter Thirteen of the *Bhagavad-gītā* (13.8–12), one should culture knowledge in the following way:

(1) One should become a perfect gentleman and

learn to give proper respect to others.

(2) One should not pose himself as a religionist simply for name and fame.

(3) One should not become a source of anxiety to others by the actions of his body, by the thoughts of his mind, or by his words.

(4) One should learn forbearance even in the face of provocation from others.

(5) One should learn to avoid duplicity in his dealings with others.

(6) One should search out a bona fide spiritual master who can lead him gradually to the stage of spiritual realization, and one must submit himself to such a spiritual master, render him service and ask relevant questions.

(7) In order to approach the platform of self-realization, one must follow the regulative principles enjoined in the revealed scriptures.

(8) One must be fixed in the tenets of the revealed scriptures.

(9) One should completely refrain from practices which are detrimental to the interest of self-realization.

(10) One should not accept more than he requires for the maintenance of the body.

(11) One should not falsely identify himself with the gross material body, nor should one consider those who are related to his body to be his own.

(12) One should always remember that as long as he has a material body he must face the miseries of repeated birth, old age, disease and death. There is no use in making plans to get rid of these miseries of the material body. The best course is to find out the

means by which one may regain his spiritual identity.

(13) One should not be attached to more than the necessities of life required for spiritual advancement.

(14) One should not be more attached to wife, children and home than the revealed scriptures ordain.

(15) One should not be happy or distressed over desirables and undesirables, knowing that such feelings are just created by the mind.

(16) One should become an unalloyed devotee of the Personality of Godhead, Śrī Kṛṣṇa, and serve Him with rapt attention.

(17) One should develop a liking for residence in a secluded place with a calm and quiet atmosphere favorable for spiritual culture, and one should avoid congested places where nondevotees congregate.

(18) One should become a scientist or philosopher and conduct research into spiritual knowledge, recognizing that spiritual knowledge is permanent whereas material knowledge ends with the death of the body.

These eighteen items combine to form a gradual process by which real knowledge can be developed. Except for these, all other methods are considered to be in the category of nescience. Śrīla Bhaktivinoda Ṭhākura, a great *ācārya,* maintained that all forms of material knowledge are merely external features of the illusory energy and that by culturing them one becomes no better than an ass. This same principle is found here in *Śrī Īśopaniṣad.* By advancement of material knowledge, modern man is simply being converted into an ass. Some materialistic politicians in spiritual guise decry the present system of civilization as satanic, but unfortunately they do not care about the culture of real knowledge as it is described in the *Bhagavad-gītā*. Thus they cannot change the satanic situation.

In the modern society, even a boy thinks himself self-sufficient and pays no respect to elderly men. Due to the wrong type of education being imparted in our universities, boys all over the world are giving their elders headaches. Thus *Śrī Īśopaniṣad* very strongly warns that the culture of nescience is different from that of knowledge. The universities are, so to speak, centers of nescience only; consequently scientists are busy discovering lethal weapons to wipe out the existence of other countries. University students today are not given instructions in the regulative principles of *brahmacarya* (celibate student life), nor do they have any faith in any scriptural injunctions. Religious principles are taught for the sake of name and fame only and not for the sake of practical action. Thus there is animosity not only in social and political fields but in the field of religion as well.

Nationalism has developed in different parts of the world due to the cultivation of nescience by the general people. No one considers that this tiny earth is just a lump of matter floating in immeasurable space along with many other lumps. In comparison to the vastness of space, these material lumps are like dust particles in the air. Because God has kindly made these lumps of matter complete in themselves, they are perfectly equipped with all necessities for floating in space. The drivers of our spaceships may be very proud of their achievements, but they do not consider the supreme driver of these greater, more gigantic spaceships called planets.

There are innumerable suns and innumerable planetary systems also. As infinitesimal parts and parcels of the Supreme Lord, we small creatures are trying to dominate these unlimited planets. Thus we take repeated birth and death and are generally frustrated by old age and disease. The span of human life is scheduled for about a hundred years, although it is gradually decreasing to twenty or thirty years. Thanks to the culture of nescience, befooled men have created their own nations within these planets in order to grasp sense enjoyment more effectively for these few years. Such foolish people draw up various plans to render national demarcations perfectly, a task that is totally impossible. Yet for this purpose each and every nation has become a source of anxiety for others. More than fifty percent of a nation's energy is devoted to defense measures and thus spoiled. No one cares for the cultivation of real knowledge, yet people are falsely proud of being advanced in both material and spiritual knowledge.

Śrī Īśopaniṣad warns us of this faulty type of education, and the *Bhagavad-gītā* gives instructions as to the development of real knowledge. This *mantra* states that the instructions of *vidyā* (knowledge) must be acquired from a *dhīra.* A *dhīra* is one who is not disturbed by material illusion. No one can be undisturbed unless he is perfectly spiritually realized, at which time one neither hankers nor laments for anything. A *dhīra* realizes that the material body and mind he has acquired by chance through material association are but foreign elements; therefore he simply makes the best use of a bad bargain.

The material body and mind are bad bargains for the spiritual living entity. The living entity has actual functions in the living, spiritual world, but this material world is dead. As long as the living spiritual sparks manipulate the dead lumps of matter, the dead world appears to be a living world. Actually it is the living souls, the parts and parcels of the supreme living being, who move the world. The *dhīras* have come to know all these facts by hearing them from superior authorities and have realized this knowledge by following the regulative principles.

To follow the regulative principles, one must take shelter of a bona fide spiritual master. The transcendental message and regulative principles come down from the spiritual master to the disciple. Such knowledge does not come in the hazardous way of nescient education. One can become a *dhīra* only by submissively hearing from a bona fide spiritual master. Arjuna, for example, became a *dhīra* by submissively hearing from Lord Kṛṣṇa, the Personality of Godhead Himself. Thus the perfect disciple must be like Arjuna, and the spiritual master must be as good as the Lord Himself. This is the process of learning *vidyā* (knowledge) from the *dhīra* (the undisturbed).

An *adhīra* (one who has not undergone the training of a *dhīra*) cannot be an instructive leader. Modern politicians who pose themselves as *dhīras* are actually *adhīras,* and one cannot expect perfect knowledge from them. They are simply busy seeing to their own remuneration in dollars and cents. How, then, can they lead the mass of people to the right path of self-realization? Thus one must hear submissively from a *dhīra* in order to attain actual education.

Mantra Eleven

विद्यां चाविद्यां च यस्तद् वेदोभयꣳ सह ।
अविद्यया मृत्युं तीर्त्वा विद्ययामृतमश्नुते ॥ ११ ॥

vidyāṁ cāvidyāṁ ca yas
tad vedobhayaṁ saha
avidyayā mṛtyuṁ tīrtvā
vidyayāmṛtam aśnute

vidyām—knowledge in fact; *ca*—and; *avidyām*—nescience; *ca*—and; *yaḥ*—a person who; *tat*—that; *veda*—knows; *ubhayam*—both; *saha*—simultaneously; *avidyayā*—by culture of nescience; *mṛtyum*—repeated death; *tīrtvā*—transcending; *vidyayā*—by culture of knowledge; *amṛtam*—deathlessness; *aśnute*—enjoys.

TRANSLATION

Only one who can learn the process of nescience and that of transcendental knowledge side by side can transcend the influence of repeated birth and death and enjoy the full blessings of immortality.

PURPORT

Since the creation of the material world, everyone has been trying to attain a permanent life, but the laws of nature are so cruel that no one has been able to avoid the hand of death. No one wants to die, nor does anyone want to become old or diseased. The law of nature, however, does not allow anyone immunity from old age, disease or death. Nor has the advancement of material knowledge solved these problems. Material science can discover the nuclear bomb to accelerate the process of death, but it cannot discover anything that can protect man from the cruel hands of old age, disease and death.

From the *Purāṇas* we learn of the activities of Hiraṇyakaśipu, a king who was very much advanced materially. Wanting to conquer cruel death by his material acquisitions and the strength of his nescience, he underwent a type of meditation so severe that the inhabitants of all the planetary systems became disturbed by his mystic powers. He forced the creator of the universe, the demigod Brahmā, to come down to him. He then asked Brahmā for the benediction of becoming *amara,* by which one does not die. Brahmā said that he could not award the benediction because even he, the material creator who rules all planets, is not *amara.* As confirmed in the *Bhagavad-gītā* (8.17), Brahmā lives a long time, but that does not mean he is immortal.

Hiraṇya means "gold," and *kaśipu* means "soft bed." This cunning gentleman Hiraṇyakaśipu was interested in these two things—money and women—and he wanted to enjoy them by becoming immortal. He asked from Brahmā many benedictions in hopes of indirectly fulfilling his desire to become immortal. Since Brahmā told him that he could not grant the gift of immortality, Hiraṇyakaśipu requested that he not be killed by any man, animal, god or any other living being within the 8,400,000 species. He also asked that he not die on land, in the air or water, or by any weapon. In this way Hiraṇyakaśipu foolishly thought these guarantees would save him from death. Ultimately, however, although Brahmā granted him all these benedictions, he was killed by the Personality of Godhead in the form of Nṛsiṁha, the Lord's half-lion, half-man incarnation, and no weapon was used to kill him, for he was killed by the Lord's nails. Nor was he killed on the land, in the air or in the water, for he was killed on the lap of that wonderful living being, Nṛsiṁha, who was beyond his conception.

The whole point here is that even Hiraṇyakaśipu, the most powerful of materialists, could not become deathless by his various plans. What, then, can be accomplished by the tiny Hiraṇyakaśipus of today, whose plans are throttled from moment to moment?

Śrī Īśopaniṣad instructs us not to make one-sided attempts to win the struggle for existence. Everyone is struggling hard for existence, but the laws of material nature are so hard and fast that they do not allow anyone to surpass them. In order to attain a permanent life, one must be prepared to go back to Godhead.

The process by which one goes back to Godhead is a different branch of knowledge, and it has to be learned from revealed Vedic scriptures such as the *Upaniṣads, Vedānta-sūtra, Bhagavad-gītā* and *Śrīmad-Bhāgavatam.* To become happy in this life and attain a permanent blissful life after leaving this material body, one must study this sacred literature and obtain transcendental knowledge. The conditioned living being has forgotten his eternal relationship with God and has mistakenly accepted the temporary place of his birth as all in all. The Lord has kindly delivered the above-mentioned scriptures in India and other scriptures in other countries to remind the forgetful human being that his home is not here in this material world. The living being is a spiritual entity, and he can be happy only by returning to his spiritual home.

From His kingdom the Personality of Godhead sends His bona fide servants to propagate this message by which one can return to Godhead, and sometimes the Lord comes Himself to do this work. Since all living beings are His beloved sons, His parts and parcels, God is more sorry than we ourselves to see the sufferings we are constantly undergoing in this material condition. The miseries of this material world serve to indirectly remind us of our incompatibility with dead matter. Intelligent living entities generally take note of these reminders and engage themselves in the culture of *vidyā,* or transcendental knowledge. Human life is the best opportunity for the culture of spiritual knowledge, and a human being who does not take advantage of this opportunity is called a *narādhama,* the lowest of human beings.

The path of *avidyā,* or advancement of material knowledge for sense gratification, is the path of repeated birth and death. As he exists spiritually, the living entity has no birth or death. Birth and death apply to the outward covering of the spirit soul, the body. Death is compared to the taking off and birth to the putting on of outward garments. Foolish human beings who are grossly absorbed in the culture of *avidyā,* nescience, do not mind this cruel process. Enamored with the beauty of the illusory energy, they undergo the same miseries repeatedly and do not learn any lessons from the laws of nature.

Therefore the culture of *vidyā,* or transcendental knowledge, is essential for the human being. Sense enjoyment in the diseased material condition must be restricted as far as possible. Unrestricted sense enjoyment in this bodily condition is the path of ignorance and death. The living entities are not without spiritual senses; every living being in his original, spiritual form has all the senses, which are now materially manifested, being covered by the material body and mind. The activities of the material senses are perverted reflections of the activities of the original, spiritual senses. In his diseased condition, the spirit soul engages in material activities under the material covering. Real sense enjoyment is possible only when the disease of materialism is removed. In our pure spiritual form, free from all material contamination, real enjoyment of the senses is possible. A patient must regain his health before he can truly enjoy sense pleasure again. Thus the aim of human life should not be to enjoy perverted sense enjoyment but to cure the material disease. Aggravation of the material disease is no sign of knowledge, but a sign of *avidyā,* ignorance. For good health, a person should not increase his fever from 105 degrees to 107 degrees but should reduce his temperature to the normal 98.6. That should be the aim of human life. The modern trend of material civilization is to increase the temperature of the feverish material condition, which has reached the point of 107 degrees in the form of atomic energy.

Meanwhile, the foolish politicians are crying that at any moment the world may go to hell. That is the result of the advancement of material knowledge and the neglect of the most important part of life, the culture of spiritual knowledge. *Śrī Īśopaniṣad* herein warns that we must not follow this dangerous path leading to death. On the contrary, we must develop the culture of spiritual knowledge so that we may become completely free from the cruel hands of death.

This does not mean that all activities for the maintenance of the body should be stopped. There is no question of stopping activities, just as there is no question of wiping out one's temperature altogether when trying to recover from a disease. "To make the best use of a bad bargain" is the appropriate expression. The culture of spiritual knowledge necessitates the help of the body and mind; therefore maintenance of the body and mind is required if we are to reach our goal. The normal temperature should be maintained at 98.6 degrees, and the great sages and saints of India have attempted to do this by a balanced program of spiritual and material knowledge. They never allow the misuse of human intelligence for diseased sense gratification.

Human activities diseased by a tendency toward sense gratification have been regulated in the *Vedas* under the principles of salvation. This system employs religion, economic development, sense gratification and salvation, but at the present moment people have no interest in religion or salvation. They have only one aim in life—sense gratification—and in order to achieve this end they make plans for economic development. Misguided men think that religion should be maintained because it contributes to economic development, which is required for sense gratification. Thus in order to guarantee further sense gratification after death, in heaven, there is some system of religious observance. But this is not the purpose of religion. The path of religion is actually meant for self-realization, and economic development is required just to maintain the body in a sound, healthy condition. A man should lead a healthy life with a sound mind just to realize *vidyā,* true knowledge, which is the aim of human life. This life is not meant for working like an ass or for culturing *avidyā* for sense gratification.

The path of *vidyā* is most perfectly presented in *Śrīmad-Bhāgavatam,* which directs a human being to utilize his life to inquire into the Absolute Truth. The Absolute Truth is realized step by step as Brahman, Paramātmā and finally Bhagavān, the Personality of Godhead. The Absolute Truth is realized by the broadminded man who has attained knowledge and detachment by following the eighteen principles of the *Bhagavad-gītā* described in the purport to Mantra Ten. The central purpose of these eighteen principles is the attainment of transcendental devotional service to the Personality of Godhead. Therefore all classes of men are encouraged to learn the art of devotional service to the Lord.

The guaranteed path to the aim of *vidyā* is described by Śrīla Rūpa Gosvāmī in his *Bhakti-rasāmṛta-sindhu,* which we have presented in English as *The Nectar of Devotion.* The culture of *vidyā* is summarized in *Śrīmad-Bhāgavatam* (1.2.14) in the following words:

tasmād ekena manasā
bhagavān sātvatāṁ patiḥ
śrotavyaḥ kīrtitavyaś ca
dhyeyaḥ pūjyaś ca nityadā

"Therefore, with one-pointed attention one should constantly hear about, glorify, remember and worship the Personality of Godhead, who is the protector of the devotees."

Unless religion, economic development and sense gratification aim toward the attainment of devotional service to the Lord, they are all simply different forms of nescience, as *Śrī Īśopaniṣad* indicates in the following *mantras.*

Mantra Twelve

अन्धं तमः प्रविशन्ति येऽसम्भूतिमुपासते ।
ततो भूय इव ते तमो य उ सम्भूत्याँ रताः ॥ १२ ॥

andhaṁ tamaḥ praviśanti
ye 'sambhūtim upāsate
tato bhūya iva te tamo
ya u sambhūtyāṁ ratāḥ

andham—ignorance; *tamaḥ*—darkness; *praviśanti*—enter into; *ye*—those who; *asambhūtim*—demigods; *upāsate*—worship; *tataḥ*—than that; *bhūyaḥ*—still more; *iva*—like that; *te*—those; *tamaḥ*—darkness; *ye*—who; *u*—also; *sambhūtyām*—in the Absolute; *ratāḥ*—engaged.

TRANSLATION

Those who are engaged in the worship of demigods enter into the darkest region of ignorance, and still more so do the worshipers of the impersonal Absolute.

PURPORT

The Sanskrit word *asambhūti* refers to those who have no independent existence. *Sambhūti* is the Absolute Personality of Godhead, who is absolutely independent of everything. In the *Bhagavad-gītā* (10.2), the Absolute Personality of Godhead, Śrī Kṛṣṇa, states:

na me viduḥ sura-gaṇā
prabhavaṁ na maharṣayaḥ
aham ādir hi devānāṁ
maharṣīṇāṁ ca sarvaśaḥ

"Neither the hosts of demigods nor the great sages know My origin or opulences, for in every respect I am the source of the demigods and sages." Thus Kṛṣṇa is the origin of the powers delegated to demigods, great sages and mystics. Although they are endowed with great powers, these powers are limited, and thus it is very difficult for them to know how Kṛṣṇa Himself appears by His own internal potency in the form of a man.

Many philosophers and great *ṛṣis,* or mystics, try to distinguish the Absolute from the relative by their tiny brain power. This can only help them reach the negative conception of the Absolute without realizing any positive trace of the Absolute. Definition of the Absolute by negation is not complete. Such negative definitions lead one to create a concept of one's own; thus one imagines that the Absolute must be formless and without qualities. Such negative qualities are simply the reversals of relative, material qualities and are therefore also relative. By conceiving of the Absolute in this way, one can at the utmost reach the impersonal effulgence of God, known as Brahman, but one cannot make further progress to Bhagavān, the Personality of Godhead.

Such mental speculators do not know that the Absolute Personality of Godhead is Kṛṣṇa, that the impersonal Brahman is the glaring effulgence of His transcendental body, or that the Paramātmā, the Supersoul, is His all-pervading plenary representation. Nor do they know that Kṛṣṇa has His eternal form with its transcendental qualities of eternal bliss and knowledge. The dependent demigods and great sages imperfectly consider Him to be a powerful demigod, and they consider the Brahman effulgence to be the Absolute Truth. But the devotees of Kṛṣṇa, by dint of their surrendering unto Him and their unalloyed devotion, can know that He is the Absolute Person and that everything emanates from Him. Such devotees continuously render loving service unto Kṛṣṇa, the fountainhead of everything.

In the *Bhagavad-gītā* (7.20, 23) it is said that only unintelligent, bewildered persons driven by a strong desire for sense gratification worship the demigods for the temporary relief of temporary problems. Since the living being is materially entangled, he has to be relieved from material bondage entirely to attain permanent relief on the spiritual plane, where eternal bliss, life and knowledge exist. *Śrī Īśopaniṣad* therefore instructs that we should not seek temporary relief of our difficulties by worshiping the dependent demigods, who can bestow only temporary benefit. Rather, we must worship the Absolute Personality of Godhead, Kṛṣṇa, who is all-attractive and who can bestow upon us complete freedom from material bondage by taking us back home, back to Godhead.

It is stated in the *Bhagavad-gītā* (7.23) that the

worshipers of the demigods can go to the planets of the demigods. The moon worshipers can go to the moon, the sun worshipers to the sun, etc. Modern scientists are now venturing to the moon with the help of rockets, but this is not really a new attempt. With their advanced consciousness, human beings are naturally inclined to travel in outer space and to reach other planets, either by spaceships, mystic powers or demigod worship. In the Vedic scriptures it is said that one can reach other planets by any one of these three ways, but the most common way is by worshiping the demigod presiding over a particular planet. In this way one can reach the moon planet, the sun planet and even Brahmaloka, the topmost planet in this universe. However, all planets in the material universe are temporary residences; the only permanent planets are the Vaikuṇṭhalokas. These are found in the spiritual sky, where the Personality of Godhead Himself predominates. As Lord Kṛṣṇa states in the *Bhagavad-gītā* (8.16):

ābrahma-bhuvanāl lokāḥ
punar āvartino 'rjuna
mām upetya tu kaunteya
punar janma na vidyate

"From the highest planet in the material world down to the lowest, all are places of misery wherein repeated birth and death take place. But one who attains My abode, O son of Kuntī, never takes birth again."

Śrī Īśopaniṣad points out that one who worships the demigods and attains to their material planets still remains in the darkest region of the universe. The whole universe is covered by the gigantic material elements; it is just like a coconut covered by a shell and half-filled with water. Since its covering is airtight, the darkness within is dense, and therefore the sun and the moon are required for illumination. Outside the universe is the vast and unlimited *brahmajyoti* expansion, which is filled with Vaikuṇṭhalokas. The biggest and highest planet in the *brahmajyoti* is Kṛṣṇaloka, or Goloka Vṛndāvana, where the Supreme Personality of Godhead, Śrī Kṛṣṇa Himself, resides. Lord Śrī Kṛṣṇa never leaves Kṛṣṇaloka. Although He dwells there with His eternal associates, He is omnipresent throughout the complete material and spiritual cosmic manifestations. This fact has already been explained in Mantra Four. The Lord is present everywhere, just like the sun, yet He is situated in one place, just as the sun is situated in its own undeviating orbit.

The problems of life cannot be solved simply by going to the moon planet or to some other planet above or below it. Therefore *Śrī Īśopaniṣad* advises us not to bother with any destination within this dark material universe, but to try to get out of it and reach the effulgent kingdom of God. There are many pseudo worshipers who become religionists only for the sake of name and fame. Such pseudo religionists do not wish to get out of this universe and reach the spiritual sky. They only want to maintain the status quo in the material world under the garb of worshiping the Lord. The atheists and impersonalists lead such foolish pseudo religionists into the darkest regions by preaching the cult of atheism. The atheist directly denies the existence of the Supreme Personality of Godhead, and the impersonalists support the atheists by stressing the impersonal aspect of the Supreme Lord. Thus far we have not come across any *mantra* in *Śrī Īśopaniṣad* in which the Supreme Personality of Godhead is denied. It is said that He can run faster than anyone. Those who are running after other planets are certainly persons, and if the Lord can run faster than all of them, how can He be impersonal? The impersonal conception of the Supreme Lord is another form of ignorance, arising from an imperfect conception of the Absolute Truth.

The ignorant pseudo religionists and the manufacturers of so-called incarnations who directly violate the Vedic injunctions are liable to enter into the darkest region of the universe because they mislead those who follow them. These impersonalists generally pose themselves as incarnations of God to foolish persons who have no knowledge of Vedic wisdom. If such foolish men have any knowledge at all, it is more dangerous in their hands than ignorance itself. Such impersonalists do not even worship the demigods according to the scriptural recommendations. In the scriptures there are recommendations for worshiping demigods under certain circumstances, but at the same time these scriptures state that there is normally no need for this. In the *Bhagavad-gītā* (7.23) it is clearly stated that the results derived from worshiping the demigods are not permanent. Since the entire material universe is impermanent, whatever is achieved within the darkness of material existence is also impermanent. The question is how to obtain real and permanent life.

His Divine Grace
A. C. Bhaktivedanta Swami Prabhupāda
Founder-Ācārya
of the International Society for Krishna Consciousness

Yogīs who meditate on the Supersoul in the heart can realize that form when they achieve *samādhi,* complete absorption of the mind. But theirs is still only a partial realization of the Absolute Truth. To realize the Absolute in full, one must practice *bhakti-yoga,* Kṛṣṇa consciousness. (p. 14)

As the embodied soul continuously passes, in this body, from childhood to youth to old age, the soul similarly passes into another body at death. The purpose of human life is to stop this painful process. (pp. 30–31)

To create the cosmos, Lord Kṛṣṇa expands Himself as Mahā-Viṣṇu, from whose body emanate the countless universes. (p. 113)

The Lord states that as soon as one reaches Him by devotional service—which is the one and only way to approach the Personality of Godhead—one attains complete freedom from the bondage of birth and death. In other words, the path of salvation from the material clutches fully depends on the principles of knowledge and detachment gained from serving the Lord. The pseudo religionists have neither knowledge nor detachment from material affairs, for most of them want to live in the golden shackles of material bondage under the shadow of philanthropic activities disguised as religious principles. By a false display of religious sentiments, they present a show of devotional service while indulging in all sorts of immoral activities. In this way they pass as spiritual masters and devotees of God. Such violators of religious principles have no respect for the authoritative *ācāryas,* the holy teachers in the strict disciplic succession. They ignore the Vedic injunction *ācāryopāsana*—"One must worship the *ācārya*"—and Kṛṣṇa's statement in the *Bhagavad-gītā* (4.2) *evaṁ paramparā-prāptam,* "This supreme science of God is received through the disciplic succession." Instead, to mislead the people in general they themselves become so-called *ācāryas,* but they do not even follow the principles of the *ācāryas.*

These rogues are the most dangerous elements in human society. Because there is no religious government, they escape punishment by the law of the state. They cannot, however, escape the law of the Supreme, who has clearly declared in the *Bhagavad-gītā* that envious demons in the garb of religious propagandists shall be thrown into the darkest regions of hell (Bg. 16.19–20). *Śrī Īśopaniṣad* confirms that these pseudo religionists are heading toward the most obnoxious place in the universe after the completion of their spiritual master business, which they conduct simply for sense gratification.

Mantra Thirteen

अन्यदेवाहुः सम्भवादन्यदाहुरसम्भवात् ।
इति शुश्रुम धीराणां ये नस्तद् विचचक्षिरे ॥ १३ ॥

anyad evāhuḥ sambhavād
anyad āhur asambhavāt
iti śuśruma dhīrāṇāṁ
ye nas tad vicacakṣire

anyat—different; *eva*—certainly; *āhuḥ*—it is said; *sambhavāt*—by worshiping the Supreme Lord, the cause of all causes; *anyat*—different; *āhuḥ*—it is said; *asambhavāt*—by worshiping what is not the Supreme; *iti*—thus; *śuśruma*—I heard it; *dhīrāṇām*—from the undisturbed authorities; *ye*—who; *naḥ*—unto us; *tat*—about that subject matter; *vicacakṣire*—perfectly explained.

TRANSLATION

It is said that one result is obtained by worshiping the supreme cause of all causes and that another result is obtained by worshiping what is not supreme. All this is heard from the undisturbed authorities, who clearly explained it.

PURPORT

The system of hearing from undisturbed authorities

is approved in this *mantra.* Unless one hears from a bona fide *ācārya,* who is never disturbed by the changes of the material world, one cannot have the real key to transcendental knowledge. The bona fide spiritual master, who has also heard the *śruti-mantras,* or Vedic knowledge, from his undisturbed *ācārya,* never presents anything that is not mentioned in the Vedic literature. In the *Bhagavad-gītā* (9.25) it is clearly said that those who worship the *pitṛs,* or forefathers, attain the planets of the forefathers, that the gross materialists who make plans to remain here stay in this world, and that the devotees of the Lord who worship none but Lord Kṛṣṇa, the supreme cause of all causes, reach Him in His spiritual sky. Here also in *Śrī Īśopaniṣad* it is verified that one achieves different results by different modes of worship. If we worship the Supreme Lord, we will certainly reach Him in His eternal abode, and if we worship demigods like the sun-god or moon-god, we can reach their respective planets without a doubt. And if we wish to remain on this wretched planet with our planning commissions and our stopgap political adjustments, we can certainly do that also.

Nowhere in authentic scriptures is it said that one will ultimately reach the same goal by doing anything or worshiping anyone. Such foolish theories are offered by self-made "spiritual masters" who have no connection with the *paramparā,* the bona fide system of disciplic succession. The bona fide spiritual master cannot say that all paths lead to the same goal and that anyone can attain this goal by his own mode of worship of the demigods or of the Supreme or whatever. Any common man can very easily understand that a person can reach his destination only when he has purchased a ticket for that destination. A person who has purchased a ticket for Calcutta can reach Calcutta, but not Bombay. But the so-called spiritual masters say that any and all paths will take one to the supreme goal. Such mundane and compromising offers attract many foolish creatures, who become puffed up with their manufactured methods of spiritual realization. The Vedic instructions, however, do not uphold them. Unless one has received knowledge from the bona fide spiritual master who is in the recognized line of disciplic succession, one cannot have the real thing as it is. Kṛṣṇa tells Arjuna in the *Bhagavad-gītā* (4.2):

evaṁ paramparā-prāptam
imaṁ rājarṣayo viduḥ
sa kāleneha mahatā
yogo naṣṭaḥ parantapa

"This supreme science was thus received through the chain of disciplic succession, and the saintly kings understood it in that way. But in course of time the succession was broken, and therefore the science as it is appears to be lost."

When Lord Śrī Kṛṣṇa was present on this earth, the *bhakti-yoga* principles defined in the *Bhagavad-gītā* had become distorted; therefore the Lord had to reestablish the disciplic system beginning with Arjuna, who was the most confidential friend and devotee of the Lord. The Lord clearly told Arjuna (Bg. 4.3) that it was because Arjuna was His devotee and friend that he could understand the principles of the *Bhagavad-gītā*. In other words, only the Lord's devotee and friend can understand the *Gītā*. This also means that only one who follows the path of Arjuna can understand the *Bhagavad-gītā*.

At the present moment there are many interpreters and translators of this sublime dialogue who care nothing for Lord Kṛṣṇa or Arjuna. Such interpreters explain the verses of the *Bhagavad-gītā* in their own way and postulate all sorts of rubbish in the name of the *Gītā*. Such interpreters believe neither in Śrī Kṛṣṇa nor in His eternal abode. How, then, can they explain the *Bhagavad-gītā*?

Kṛṣṇa clearly says that only those who have lost their sense worship the demigods for paltry rewards (Bg. 7.20, 23). Ultimately He advises that one give up all other ways and modes of worship and fully surrender unto Him alone (Bg. 18.66). Only those who are cleansed of all sinful reactions can have such unflinching faith in the Supreme Lord. Others will continue hovering on the material platform with their paltry ways of worship and thus will be misled from the real path under the false impression that all paths lead to the same goal.

In this *mantra* of *Śrī Īśopaniṣad* the word *sambhavāt,* "by worship of the supreme cause," is very significant. Lord Kṛṣṇa is the original Personality of Godhead, and everything that exists has emanated from Him. In the *Bhagavad-gītā* (10.8) the Lord says,

ahaṁ sarvasya prabhavo
mattaḥ sarvaṁ pravartate
iti matvā bhajante māṁ
budhā bhāva-samanvitāḥ

"I am the source of all spiritual and material worlds.

Everything emanates from Me. The wise who perfectly know this engage in My devotional service and worship Me with all their hearts."

Here is a correct description of the Supreme Lord, given by the Lord Himself. The words *sarvasya prabhavaḥ* indicate that Kṛṣṇa is the creator of everyone, including Brahmā, Viṣṇu and Śiva. And because these three principal deities of the material world are created by the Lord, the Lord is the creator of all that exists in the material and spiritual worlds. In the *Atharva Veda* (*Gopāla-tāpanī Upaniṣad* 1.24) it is similarly said, "He who existed before the creation of Brahmā and who enlightened Brahmā with Vedic knowledge is Lord Śrī Kṛṣṇa." Similarly, the *Nārāyaṇa Upaniṣad* (1) states, "Then the Supreme Person, Nārāyaṇa, desired to create all living beings. Thus from Nārāyaṇa, Brahmā was born. Nārāyaṇa created all the Prajāpatis. Nārāyaṇa created Indra. Nārāyaṇa created the eight Vasus. Nārāyaṇa created the eleven Rudras. Nārāyaṇa created the twelve Ādityas." Since Nārāyaṇa is a plenary manifestation of Lord Kṛṣṇa, Nārāyaṇa and Kṛṣṇa are one and the same. The *Nārāyaṇa Upaniṣad* (4) also states, "Devakī's son [Kṛṣṇa] is the Supreme Lord." The identity of Nārāyaṇa with the supreme cause has also been accepted and confirmed by Śrīpāda Śaṅkarācārya, even though Śaṅkara does not belong to the Vaiṣṇava, or personalist, cult. The *Atharva Veda* (*Mahā Upaniṣad* 1) also states, "Only Nārāyaṇa existed in the beginning, when neither Brahmā, nor Śiva, nor fire, nor water, nor stars, nor sun, nor moon existed. The Lord does not remain alone but creates as He desires." Kṛṣṇa Himself states in the

Mokṣa-dharma, "I created the Prajāpatis and the Rudras. They do not have complete knowledge of Me because they are covered by My illusory energy." It is also stated in the *Varāha Purāṇa:* "Nārāyaṇa is the Supreme Personality of Godhead, and from Him the four-headed Brahmā was manifested, as well as Rudra, who later became omniscient."

Thus all Vedic literature confirms that Nārāyaṇa, or Kṛṣṇa, is the cause of all causes. In the *Brahma-saṁhitā* (5.1) also it is said that the Supreme Lord is Śrī Kṛṣṇa, Govinda, the delighter of every living being and the primeval cause of all causes. The really learned persons know this from evidence given by the great sages and the *Vedas,* and thus they decide to worship Lord Kṛṣṇa as all in all. Such persons are called *budha,* or really learned, because they worship only Kṛṣṇa.

The conviction that Kṛṣṇa is all in all is established when one hears the transcendental message from the undisturbed *ācārya* with faith and love. One who has no faith in or love for Lord Kṛṣṇa cannot be convinced of this simple truth. Those who are faithless are described in the *Bhagavad-gītā* (9.11) as *mūḍhas*—fools or asses. It is said that the *mūḍhas* deride the Personality of Godhead because they do not have complete knowledge from the undisturbed *ācārya.* One who is disturbed by the whirlpool of material energy is not qualified to become an *ācārya.*

Before hearing the *Bhagavad-gītā,* Arjuna was disturbed by the material whirlpool, by his affection for his family, society and community. Thus Arjuna wanted to become a philanthropic, nonviolent man of the world. But when he became *budha* by hearing the Vedic knowledge of the *Bhagavad-gītā* from the Supreme Person, he changed his decision and became a worshiper of Lord Śrī Kṛṣṇa, who had Himself arranged the Battle of Kurukṣetra. Arjuna worshiped the Lord by fighting with his so-called relatives, and in this way he became a pure devotee of the Lord. Such accomplishments are possible only when one worships the real Kṛṣṇa and not some fabricated "Kṛṣṇa" invented by foolish men who are without knowledge of the intricacies of the science of Kṛṣṇa described in the *Bhagavad-gītā* and *Śrīmad-Bhāgavatam.*

According to the *Vedānta-sūtra, sambhūta* is the source of birth and sustenance, as well as the reservoir that remains after annihilation (*janmādy asya yataḥ*). The *Śrīmad-Bhāgavatam,* the natural commentary on the *Vedānta-sūtra* by the same author, maintains that the source of all emanations is not like a dead stone but is *abhijña,* or fully conscious. The primeval Lord, Śrī Kṛṣṇa, also says in the *Bhagavad-gītā* (7.26) that He is fully conscious of past, present and future and that no one, including demigods such as Śiva and Brahmā, knows Him fully. Certainly half-educated "spiritual leaders" who are disturbed by the tides of material existence cannot know Him fully. They try to make some compromise by making the mass of humanity the object of worship, but they do not know that such worship is only a myth because the masses are imperfect. The attempt by these so-called spiritual leaders is something like pouring water on the leaves of a tree instead of the root. The natural process is to pour water on the root, but such disturbed leaders are more attracted to the leaves than the root. Despite their perpetually watering the leaves, however, everything dries up for want of nourishment.

Śrī Īśopaniṣad advises us to pour water on the root, the source of all germination. Worship of the mass of humanity by rendering bodily service, which can never be perfect, is less important than service to the soul. The soul is the root that generates different types of bodies according to the law of *karma.* To serve human beings by medical aid, social help and educational facilities while at the same time cutting the throats of poor animals in slaughterhouses is no service at all to the soul, the living being.

The living being is perpetually suffering in different types of bodies from the material miseries of birth, old age, disease and death. The human form of life offers one a chance to get out of this entanglement simply by reestablishing the lost relationship between the living entity and the Supreme Lord. The Lord comes personally to teach this philosophy of surrender unto the Supreme, the *sambhūta.* Real service to humanity is rendered when one teaches surrender to and worship of the Supreme Lord with full love and energy. That is the instruction of *Śrī Īśopaniṣad* in this *mantra.*

The simple way to worship the Supreme Lord in this age of disturbance is to hear and chant about His great activities. The mental speculators, however, think that the activities of the Lord are imaginary; therefore they refrain from hearing of them and invent some word jugglery without any substance to divert the attention of the innocent masses of people. Instead of hearing of the activities of Lord Kṛṣṇa, such pseudo spiritual masters advertise themselves by inducing their followers to sing about *them.* In modern times the number of such pretenders has increased considerably, and it has become a problem for the pure devotees of the Lord to save the masses of people from the unholy propaganda of these pretenders and pseudo incarnations.

The *Upaniṣads* indirectly draw our attention to the primeval Lord, Śrī Kṛṣṇa, but the *Bhagavad-gītā,* which is the summary of all the *Upaniṣads,* directly points to Śrī Kṛṣṇa. Therefore one should hear about Kṛṣṇa as He is by hearing from the *Bhagavad-gītā* or *Śrīmad-Bhāgavatam,* and in this way one's mind will gradually be cleansed of all contaminated things. *Śrīmad-Bhāgavatam* (1.2.17) says, "By hearing of the activities of the Lord, the devotee draws the attention of the Lord. Thus the Lord, being situated in the heart of every living being, helps the devotee by giving him proper directions." The *Bhagavad-gītā* (10.10) confirms this: *dadāmi buddhi-yogaṁ taṁ yena mām upayānti te.*

The Lord's inner direction cleanses the devotee's heart of all contamination produced by the material modes of passion and ignorance. Nondevotees are under the sway of passion and ignorance. One who is in passion cannot become detached from material hankering, and one who is in ignorance cannot know what he is or what the Lord is. Thus when one is in passion or ignorance, there is no chance for self-realization, however much one may play the part of a religionist. For a devotee, the modes of passion and ignorance are removed by the grace of the Lord. In this way the devotee becomes situated in the quality of goodness, the sign of a perfect *brāhmaṇa*. Anyone can qualify as a *brāhmaṇa* if he follows the path of devotional service under the guidance of a bona fide spiritual master. *Śrīmad-Bhāgavatam* (2.4.18) also says:

kirāta-hūṇāndhra-pulinda-pulkaśā
ābhīra-śumbhā yavanāḥ khasādayaḥ
ye 'nye ca pāpā yad-apāśrayāśrayāḥ
śudhyanti tasmai prabhaviṣṇave namaḥ

Any lowborn person can be purified by the guidance of a pure devotee of the Lord, for the Lord is extraordinarily powerful.

When one attains brahminical qualifications, he becomes happy and enthusiastic to render devotional service to the Lord. Automatically the science of God is unveiled before him. By knowing the science of God, one gradually becomes freed from material attachments, and one's doubtful mind becomes crystal clear by the grace of the Lord. One who attains this stage is a liberated soul and can see the Lord in every step of life. This is the perfection of *sambhava,* as described in this *mantra* of *Śrī Īśopaniṣad.*

Mantra Fourteen

सम्भूतिं च विनाशं च यस्तद् वेदोभयꣳ सह ।
विनाशेन मृत्युं तीर्त्वा सम्भूत्यामृतमश्नुते ॥ १४ ॥

sambhūtiṁ ca vināśaṁ ca
yas tad vedobhayaṁ saha
vināśena mṛtyuṁ tīrtvā
sambhūtyāmṛtam aśnute

sambhūtim—the eternal Personality of Godhead, His transcendental name, form, pastimes, qualities and paraphernalia, the variegatedness of His abode, etc.; *ca*—and; *vināśam*—the temporary material manifestation of demigods, men, animals, etc., with their false names, fame, etc.; *ca*—also; *yaḥ*—one who; *tat*—that; *veda*—knows; *ubhayam*—both; *saha*—along with; *vināśena*—with everything liable to be vanquished; *mṛtyum*—death; *tīrtvā*—surpassing; *sambhūtyā*—in the eternal kingdom of God; *amṛtam*—deathlessness; *aśnute*—enjoys.

TRANSLATION

One should know perfectly the Personality of Godhead Śrī Kṛṣṇa and His transcendental name, form, qualities and pastimes, as well as the temporary material creation with its temporary demigods, men and

animals. When one knows these, he surpasses death and the ephemeral cosmic manifestation with it, and in the eternal kingdom of God he enjoys his eternal life of bliss and knowledge.

PURPORT

By its so-called advancement of knowledge, human civilization has created many material things, including spaceships and atomic energy. Yet it has failed to create a situation in which people need not die, take birth again, become old or suffer from disease. Whenever an intelligent man raises the question of these miseries before a so-called scientist, the scientist very cleverly replies that material science is progressing and that ultimately it will be possible to render man deathless, ageless and diseaseless. Such answers prove the scientists' gross ignorance of material nature. In material nature, everyone is under the stringent laws of matter and must pass through six stages of existence: birth, growth, maintenance, production of by-products, deterioration and finally death. No one in contact with material nature can be beyond these six laws of transformation; therefore no one—whether demigod, man, animal or plant—can survive forever in the material world.

The duration of life varies according to species. Lord Brahmā, the chief living being within this material universe, lives for millions and millions of years, while a minute germ lives for some hours only. But no one in the material world can survive eternally. Things are born or created under certain conditions, they stay for some time, and, if they continue to live, they grow, procreate, gradually dwindle and finally vanish. According to these laws, even the Brahmās, of which there are millions in different universes, are all liable to death either today or tomorrow. Therefore the entire material universe is called Martyaloka, the place of death.

Material scientists and politicians are trying to make this place deathless because they have no information of the deathless spiritual nature. This is due to their ignorance of the Vedic literature, which contains full knowledge confirmed by mature transcendental experience. Unfortunately, modern man is averse to receiving knowledge from the *Vedas, Purāṇas* and other scriptures.

From the *Viṣṇu Purāṇa* (6.7.61) we receive the following information:

viṣṇu-śaktiḥ parā proktā
kṣetrajñākhyā tathā parā
avidyā-karma-saṁjñānyā
tṛtīyā śaktir iṣyate

Lord Viṣṇu, the Personality of Godhead, possesses different energies, known as *parā* (superior) and *aparā* (inferior). The living entities belong to the superior energy. The material energy, in which we are presently entangled, is the inferior energy. The material creation is made possible by this energy, which covers the living entities with ignorance (*avidyā*) and induces them to perform fruitive activities. Yet there is another part of the Lord's superior energy that is different from both this material, inferior energy and the living entities. That superior energy constitutes the eternal, deathless abode of the Lord. This is confirmed in the *Bhagavad-gītā* (8.20):

paras tasmāt tu bhāvo 'nyo
'vyakto 'vyaktāt sanātanaḥ
yaḥ sa sarveṣu bhūteṣu
naśyatsu na vinaśyati

All the material planets—upper, lower and intermediate, including the sun, moon and Venus—are scattered throughout the universe. These planets exist only during the lifetime of Brahmā. Some lower planets, however, are vanquished after the end of one day of Brahmā and are again created during the next day of Brahmā. On the upper planets, time is calculated differently. One of our years is equal to only twenty-four hours, or one day and night, on many of the upper planets. The four ages of earth (Satya, Tretā, Dvāpara and Kali) last only twelve thousand years according to the time scale of the upper planets. Such a length of time multiplied by one thousand constitutes one day of Brahmā, and one night of Brahmā is the same. Such days and nights accumulate into months and years, and Brahmā lives for one hundred such years. At the end of Brahmā's life, the complete universal manifestation is vanquished.

Those living beings who reside on higher planets like the sun and the moon, as well as those on Martyaloka, this earth planet, and also those who live on lower planets—all are merged into the waters of devastation during the night of Brahmā. During this time no living beings or species remain manifest, although spiritually they continue to exist. This unmanifested stage is called *avyakta.* Again, when the entire universe is vanquished at the end of Brahmā's lifetime, there is another *avyakta* state. But beyond these two unmanifested states is another unmanifested state, the spiritual atmosphere, or nature. There are a great number of spiritual planets in this atmosphere, and these planets exist eternally, even when all the planets within this material universe are vanquished at the end of Brahmā's life. There are many material universes, each under the jurisdiction of a Brahmā, and this cosmic manifestation within the jurisdiction of the various Brahmās is but a display of one fourth of the energy of the Lord (*ekapād-vibhūti*). This is the inferior energy. Be-yond the jurisdiction of Brahmā is the spiritual nature, which is called *tripād-vibhūti,* three fourths of the Lord's energy. This is the superior energy, or *parā-prakṛti.*

The predominating Supreme Person residing within the spiritual nature is Lord Śrī Kṛṣṇa. As confirmed in the *Bhagavad-gītā* (8.22), He can be approached only by unalloyed devotional service and not by the processes of *jñāna* (philosophy), *yoga* (mysticism) or *karma* (fruitive work). The *karmīs*, or fruitive workers, can elevate themselves to the Svargaloka planets, which include the sun and the moon. *Jñānīs* and *yogīs* can attain still higher planets, such as Maharloka, Tapoloka and Brahmaloka, and when they become still more qualified through devotional service they can enter into the spiritual nature, either the illuminating cosmic atmosphere of the spiritual sky (Brahman) or the Vaikuṇṭha planets, according to their qualification. It is certain, however, that no one can enter into the spiritual Vaikuṇṭha planets without being trained in devotional service.

On the material planets, everyone from Brahmā down to the ant is trying to lord it over material nature, and this is the material disease. As long as this material disease continues, the living entity has to undergo the process of bodily change. Whether he takes the form of a man, demigod or animal, he ultimately has to endure an unmanifested condition during the two devastations—the devastation during the night of Brahmā and the devastation at the end of Brahmā's life. If we want to put an end to this process of repeated birth and death, as well as the concomitant factors of old age and disease, we must try to enter the spiritual planets, where we can live eternally in the association of Lord Kṛṣṇa or His plenary expansions, His Nārāyaṇa forms. Lord Kṛṣṇa or His plenary expansions dominate every one of these innumerable planets, a fact confirmed in the *śruti mantras: eko vaśī sarva-gaḥ kṛṣṇa īḍyaḥ / eko 'pi san bahudhā yo 'vabhāti.* (*Gopāla-tāpanī Upaniṣad* 1.3.21)

No one can dominate Kṛṣṇa. It is the conditioned soul who tries to dominate material nature and is instead subjected to the laws of material nature and the sufferings of repeated birth and death. The Lord comes here to reestablish the principles of religion, and the basic principle is the development of an attitude of surrender to Him. This is the Lord's last instruction in the *Bhagavad-gītā* (18.66): *sarva-dharmān parityajya mām ekaṁ śaraṇaṁ vraja.* "Give up all other processes and just surrender unto Me alone." Unfortunately, foolish men have misinterpreted this prime teaching and misled the masses of people in diverse ways. People have been urged to open hospitals but not to educate themselves to enter into the spiritual kingdom by devotional service. They have been taught to take interest only in temporary relief work, which can never bring real happiness to the living entity. They start varieties of public and semi-governmental institutions to tackle the devastating power of nature, but they don't know how to pacify insurmountable nature. Many men are advertised as great scholars of the *Bhagavad-gītā,* but they overlook the *Gītā's* message, by which material nature can be pacified. Powerful nature can be pacified only by the awakening of God consciousness, as clearly pointed out in the *Bhagavad-gītā* (7.14).

In this *mantra, Śrī Īśopaniṣad* teaches that one must perfectly know both *sambhūti* (the Personality of Godhead) and *vināśa* (the temporary material manifestation), side by side. By knowing the material manifestation alone, one cannot be saved, for in the course of nature there is devastation at every moment (*ahany ahani bhūtāni gacchantīha yamālayam*). Nor can one be saved from these devastations by the opening of hospitals. One can be saved only by complete knowledge of the eternal life of bliss and awareness. The whole Vedic scheme is meant to educate men in this art of attaining eternal life. People are often misguided by temporary attractive things based on sense gratification, but service rendered to the sense objects is both misleading and degrading.

We must therefore save ourselves and our fellow man in the right way. There is no question of liking or disliking the truth. It is there. If we want to be saved from repeated birth and death, we must take to the devotional service of the Lord. There can be no compromise, for this is a matter of necessity.

Mantra Fifteen

हिरण्मयेन पात्रेण सत्यस्यापिहितं मुखम् ।
तत् त्वं पूषन्नपावृणु सत्यधर्माय दृष्टये ॥ १५ ॥

hiraṇmayena pātreṇa
satyasyāpihitaṁ mukham
tat tvaṁ pūṣann apāvṛṇu
satya-dharmāya dṛṣṭaye

hiraṇmayena—by a golden effulgence; *pātreṇa*—by a dazzling covering; *satyasya*—of the Supreme Truth; *apihitam*—covered; *mukham*—the face; *tat*—that covering; *tvam*—Yourself; *pūṣan*—O sustainer; *apāvṛṇu*—kindly remove; *satya*—pure; *dharmāya*—unto the devotee; *dṛṣṭaye*—for exhibiting.

TRANSLATION

O my Lord, sustainer of all that lives, Your real face is covered by Your dazzling effulgence. Kindly remove that covering and exhibit Yourself to Your pure devotee.

PURPORT

In the *Bhagavad-gītā* (14.27), the Lord explains His personal rays (*brahmajyoti*), the dazzling effulgence of His personal form, in this way:

brahmaṇo hi pratiṣṭhāham
amṛtasyāvyayasya ca
śāśvatasya ca dharmasya
sukhasyaikāntikasya ca

"I am the basis of the impersonal Brahman, which is immortal, imperishable and eternal and is the constitutional position of ultimate happiness." Brahman, Paramātmā and Bhagavān are three aspects of the same Absolute Truth. Brahman is the aspect most easily perceived by the beginner; Paramātmā, the Supersoul, is realized by those who have further progressed; and Bhagavān realization is the ultimate realization of the Absolute Truth. This is confirmed in the *Bhagavad-gītā* (7.7), where Lord Kṛṣṇa says that He is the ultimate concept of the Absolute Truth: *mattaḥ parataraṁ nānyat.* Therefore Kṛṣṇa is the source of the *brahmajyoti* as well as the all-pervading Paramātmā. Later in the *Bhagavad-gītā* (10.42) Kṛṣṇa further explains:

atha vā bahunaitena
kiṁ jñātena tavārjuna
viṣṭabhyāham idaṁ kṛtsnam
ekāṁśena sthito jagat

"But what need is there, Arjuna, for all this detailed knowledge? With a single fragment of Myself I pervade and support this entire universe." Thus by His one plenary expansion, the all-pervading Paramātmā, the Lord maintains the complete material cosmic creation. He also maintains all manifestations in the spiritual world. Therefore in this *śruti-mantra* of *Śrī*

Īśopaniṣad, the Lord is addressed as *pūṣan,* the ultimate maintainer.

The Personality of Godhead, Śrī Kṛṣṇa, is always filled with transcendental bliss (*ānanda-mayo 'bhyāsāt*). When He was present at Vṛndāvana in India five thousand years ago, He always remained in transcendental bliss, even from the beginning of His childhood pastimes. The killings of various demons—such as Agha, Baka, Pūtanā and Pralamba—were but pleasure excursions for Him. In His village of Vṛndāvana He enjoyed Himself with His mother, brother and friends, and when He played the role of a naughty butter thief, all His associates enjoyed celestial bliss by His stealing. The Lord's fame as a butter thief is not reproachable, for by stealing butter the Lord gave pleasure to His pure devotees. Everything the Lord did in Vṛndāvana was for the pleasure of His associates there. The Lord created these pastimes to attract the dry speculators and the acrobats of the so-called *haṭha-yoga* system who wish to find the Absolute Truth.

Of the childhood play between the Lord and His playmates, the cowherd boys, Śukadeva Gosvāmī says in *Śrīmad-Bhāgavatam* (10.12.11):

itthaṁ satāṁ brahma-sukhānubhūtyā
dāsyaṁ gatānāṁ para-daivatena
māyāśritānāṁ nara-dārakeṇa
sākaṁ vijahruḥ kṛta-puṇya-puñjāḥ

"The Personality of Godhead, who is perceived as the impersonal, blissful Brahman by the *jñānīs,* who is worshiped as the Supreme Lord by devotees in the mood of servitorship, and who is considered an ordinary human being by mundane people, played with the cowherd boys, who had attained their position after accumulating many pious activities."

Thus the Lord is always engaged in transcendental loving activities with His spiritual associates in the various relationships of *śānta* (neutrality), *dāsya* (servitorship), *sakhya* (friendship), *vātsalya* (parental affection) and *mādhurya* (conjugal love).

Since it is said that Lord Kṛṣṇa never leaves Vṛndāvana-dhāma, one may ask how He manages the affairs of the creation. This is answered in the *Bhagavad-gītā* (13.14–18): The Lord pervades the entire material creation by His plenary part known as the Paramātma, or Supersoul. Although the Lord personally has nothing to do with material creation, maintenance and destruction, He causes all these things to be done by His plenary expansion, the Paramātmā. Every living entity is known as *ātmā,* soul, and the principal *ātmā* who controls them all is Paramātmā, the Supersoul.

This system of God realization is a great science. The materialistic *sāṅkhya-yogīs* can only analyze and meditate on the twenty-four factors of the material creation, for they have very little information of the *puruṣa,* the Lord. And the impersonal transcendentalists are simply bewildered by the glaring effulgence of the *brahmajyoti.* If one wants to see the Absolute Truth in full, one has to penetrate beyond the twenty-four material elements and the glaring effulgence as well. *Śrī Īśopaniṣad* points toward this direction, praying for the removal of the *hiraṇmaya-pātra,* the dazzling covering of the Lord. Unless this covering is removed so one can perceive the real face of the Personality of Godhead, factual realization of the Absolute Truth can never be achieved.

The Paramātmā feature of the Personality of Godhead is one of three plenary expansions, or *viṣṇu-tattvas,* collectively known as the *puruṣa-avatāras.* One of these *viṣṇu-tattvas* who is within the universe is known as Kṣīrodakaśāyī Viṣṇu. He is the Viṣṇu among the three principal deities—Brahmā, Viṣṇu and Śiva—and He is the all-pervading Paramātmā in each and every individual living entity. The second *viṣṇu-tattva* within the universe is Garbhodakaśāyī Viṣṇu, the collective Supersoul within all living entities. Beyond these two is Kāraṇodakaśāyī Viṣṇu, who lies in the Causal Ocean. He is the creator of all universes. The *yoga* system teaches the serious student to meet the *viṣṇu-tattvas* after going beyond the twenty-four material elements of the cosmic creation. The culture of empiric philosophy helps one realize the impersonal *brahmajyoti,* which is the glaring effulgence of the transcendental body of Lord Śrī Kṛṣṇa. That the *brahmajyoti* is Kṛṣṇa's effulgence is confirmed in the *Bhagavad-gītā* (14.27) as well as the *Brahma-saṁhitā* (5.40):

yasya prabhā-prabhavato jagad-aṇḍa-koṭi-
koṭiṣv aśeṣa-vasudhādi vibhūti-bhinnam
tad brahma niṣkalam anantam aśeṣa-bhūtaṁ
govindam ādi-puruṣaṁ tam ahaṁ bhajāmi

"In the millions and millions of universes there are innumerable planets, and each and every one of them is different from the others by its cosmic constitution.

All of these planets are situated in a corner of the *brahmajyoti.* This *brahmajyoti* is but the personal rays of the Supreme Personality of Godhead, Govinda, whom I worship." This *mantra* from the *Brahma-saṁhitā* is spoken from the platform of factual realization of the Absolute Truth, and the *śruti-mantra* of *Śrī Īśopaniṣad* under discussion confirms this *mantra* as a process of realization. The *Īśopaniṣad mantra* is a simple prayer to the Lord to remove the *brahmajyoti* so that one can see His real face. This *brahmajyoti* effulgence is described in detail in several *mantras* of the *Muṇḍaka Upaniṣad* (2.2.10–12):

hiraṇmaye pare kośe
virajaṁ brahma niṣkalam
tac chubhraṁ jyotiṣāṁ jyotis
tad yad ātma-vido viduḥ

na tatra sūryo bhāti na candra-tārakaṁ
nemā vidyuto bhānti kuto 'yam agniḥ
tam eva bhāntam anu bhāti sarvaṁ
tasya bhāsā sarvam idaṁ vibhāti

brahmaivedam amṛtaṁ purastād brahma
paścād brahma dakṣiṇataś cottareṇa
adhaś cordhvaṁ ca prasṛtaṁ brahmai-
vedaṁ viśvam idaṁ variṣṭham

"In the spiritual realm, beyond the material covering, is the unlimited Brahman effulgence, which is free from material contamination. That effulgent white light is understood by transcendentalists to be the light of all lights. In that realm there is no need of sunshine, moonshine, fire or electricity for illumination. Indeed, whatever illumination appears in the material world is only a reflection of that supreme illumination. That Brahman is in front and in back, in the north, south, east and west, and also overhead and below. In other words, that supreme Brahman effulgence spreads throughout both the material and spiritual skies."

Perfect knowledge means knowing Kṛṣṇa as the root of this Brahman effulgence. This knowledge can be gained from such scriptures as *Śrīmad-Bhāgavatam,* which perfectly elaborates the science of Kṛṣṇa. In *Śrīmad-Bhāgavatam*, the author, Śrīla Vyāsadeva, has established that one will describe the Supreme Truth as Brahman, Paramātmā or Bhagavān according to one's realization of Him. Śrīla Vyāsadeva never states that the Supreme Truth is a *jīva,* an ordinary living entity. The living entity should never be considered the all-powerful Supreme Truth. If he were the Supreme, he would not need to pray to the Lord to remove His dazzling cover so that the living entity could see His real face.

The conclusion is that one who has no knowledge of the potencies of the Supreme Truth will realize the impersonal Brahman. Similarly, when one realizes the material potencies of the Lord but has little or no information of the spiritual potencies, he attains Paramātmā realization. Thus both Brahman and Paramātmā realization of the Absolute Truth are partial realizations. However, when one realizes the Supreme Personality of Godhead, Śrī Kṛṣṇa, in full potency after the removal of the *hiraṇmaya-pātra,* one realizes *vāsudevaḥ sarvam iti:* Lord Śrī Kṛṣṇa, who is known as Vāsudeva, is everything—Brahman, Paramātmā and Bhagavān. He is

Bhagavān, the root, and Brahman and Paramātmā are His branches.

In the *Bhagavad-gītā* (6.46–47) there is a comparative analysis of the three types of transcendentalists—the worshipers of the impersonal Brahman (*jñānīs*), the worshipers of the Paramātmā feature (*yogīs*) and the devotees of Lord Śrī Kṛṣṇa (*bhaktas*). It is stated there that the *jñānīs,* those who have cultivated Vedic knowledge, are better than ordinary fruitive workers, that the *yogīs* are still greater than the *jñānīs,* and that among all *yogīs,* those who constantly serve the Lord with all their energies are the topmost. In summary, a philosopher is better than a laboring man, a mystic is superior to a philosopher, and of all the mystic *yogīs,* he who follows *bhakti-yoga,* constantly engaging in the service of the Lord, is the highest. *Śrī Īśopaniṣad* directs us toward this perfection.

Mantra Sixteen

पूषन्नेकर्षे यम सूर्य प्राजापत्य
व्यूह रश्मीन् समूह ।
तेजो यत् ते रूपं कल्याणतमं तत्
ते पश्यामि योऽसावसौ पुरुषः सोऽहमस्मि ॥ १६ ॥

pūṣann ekarṣe yama sūrya prājāpatya
vyūha raśmīn samūha
tejo yat te rūpaṁ kalyāṇa-tamaṁ
tat te paśyāmi yo 'sāv asau puruṣaḥ so 'ham asmi

pūṣan—O maintainer; *eka-ṛṣe*—the primeval philosopher; *yama*—the regulating principle; *sūrya*—the destination of the *sūris* (great devotees); *prājāpatya*—the well-wisher of the *prajāpatis* (progenitors of mankind); *vyūha*—kindly remove; *raśmīn*—the rays; *samūha*—kindly withdraw; *tejaḥ*—effulgence; *yat*—so that; *te*—Your; *rūpam*—form; *kalyāṇa-tamam*—most auspicious; *tat*—that; *te*—Your; *paśyāmi*—I may see; *yaḥ*—one who is; *asau*—like the sun; *asau*—that; *puruṣaḥ*—Personality of Godhead; *saḥ*—myself; *aham*—I; *asmi*—am.

TRANSLATION

O my Lord, O primeval philosopher, maintainer of the universe, O regulating principle, destination of

the pure devotees, well-wisher of the progenitors of mankind, please remove the effulgence of Your transcendental rays so that I can see Your form of bliss. You are the eternal Supreme Personality of Godhead, like unto the sun, as am I.

PURPORT

The sun and its rays are one and the same qualitatively. Similarly, the Lord and the living entities are one and the same in quality. The sun is one, but the molecules of the sun's rays are innumerable. The sun's rays constitute part of the sun, and the sun and its rays conjointly constitute the complete sun. Within the sun itself resides the sun-god, and similarly within the supreme spiritual planet, Goloka Vṛndāvana, from which the *brahmajyoti* effulgence is emanating, the Lord enjoys His eternal pastimes, as verified in the *Brahma-saṁhitā* (5.29):

cintāmaṇi-prakara-sadmasu kalpa-vṛkṣa-
lakṣāvṛteṣu surabhīr abhipālayantam
lakṣmī-sahasra-śata-sambhrama-sevyamānaṁ
govindam ādi-puruṣaṁ tam ahaṁ bhajāmi

"I worship Govinda, the primeval Lord, the first progenitor, who is tending the cows fulfilling all desires in abodes filled with spiritual gems and surrounded by millions of wish-fulfilling trees. He is always served with great reverence and affection by hundreds of thousands of Lakṣmīs, or goddesses of fortune."

The *brahmajyoti* is described in the *Brahma-saṁhitā* as the rays emanating from that supreme spiritual planet, Goloka Vṛndāvana, just as the sun's rays emanate from the sun globe. Until one surpasses the glare of the *brahmajyoti*, one cannot receive information of the land of the Lord. The impersonalist philosophers, blinded as they are by the dazzling *brahmajyoti*, can realize neither the factual abode of the Lord nor His transcendental form. Limited by their poor fund of knowledge, such impersonalist thinkers cannot understand the all-blissful transcendental form of Lord Kṛṣṇa. In this prayer, therefore, *Śrī Īśopaniṣad* petitions the Lord to remove the effulgent rays of the *brahmajyoti* so that the pure devotee can see His all-blissful transcendental form.

By realizing the impersonal *brahmajyoti*, one experiences the auspicious aspect of the Supreme, and by realizing the Paramātmā, or all-pervading feature of the Supreme, one experiences an even more auspicious enlightenment. But by meeting the Personality of Godhead Himself face to face, the devotee experiences the most auspicious feature of the Supreme. Since He is addressed as the primeval philosopher and maintainer and well-wisher of the universe, the Supreme Truth cannot be impersonal. This is the verdict of *Śrī Īśopaniṣad.* The word *pūṣan* ("maintainer") is especially significant, for although the Lord maintains all beings, He specifically maintains His devotees. After surpassing the impersonal *brahmajyoti* and seeing the personal aspect of the Lord and His most auspicious eternal form, the devotee realizes the Absolute Truth in full.

In his *Bhagavat-sandarbha,* Śrīla Jīva Gosvāmī states: "The complete conception of the Absolute

Truth is realized in the Personality of Godhead because He is almighty and possesses full transcendental potencies. The full potency of the Absolute Truth is not realized in the *brahmajyoti;* therefore Brahman realization is only partial realization of the Personality of Godhead. O learned sages, the first syllable of the word *bhagavān* (*bha*) has two meanings: the first is 'one who fully maintains,' and the second is 'guardian.' The second syllable (*ga*) means 'guide,' 'leader' or 'creator.' The syllable *vān* indicates that every being lives in Him and that He also lives in every being. In other words, the transcendental sound *bhagavān* represents infinite knowledge, potency, energy, opulence, strength and influence—all without a tinge of material inebriety."

The Lord fully maintains His unalloyed devotees, and He guides them progressively on the path toward devotional perfection. As the leader of His devotees, He ultimately awards the desired results of devotional service by giving Himself to them. The devotees of the Lord see the Lord eye to eye by His causeless mercy; thus the Lord helps His devotees reach the supermost spiritual planet, Goloka Vṛndāvana. Being the creator, He can bestow all necessary qualifications upon His devotees so that they can ultimately reach Him. The Lord is the cause of all causes. In other words, since there is nothing that caused Him, He is the original cause. Consequently He enjoys His own Self by manifesting His own internal potency. The external potency is not exactly manifested by Him, for He expands Himself as the *puruṣas,* and it is in these forms that He maintains the features of the material manifestation. By such expansions, He creates, maintains and annihilates the cosmic manifestation.

The living entities are also differentiated expansions of the Lord's Self, and because some of them desire to be lords and imitate the Supreme Lord, He allows them to enter into the cosmic creation with the option to fully utilize their propensity to lord it over nature. Because of the presence of His parts and parcels, the living entities, the entire phenomenal world is stirred into action and reaction. Thus the living entities are given full facilities to lord it over material nature, but the ultimate controller is the Lord Himself in His plenary feature as Paramātmā, the Supersoul, who is one of the *puruṣas.*

Thus there is a gulf of difference between the living entity (*ātmā*) and the controlling Lord (Paramātmā), the soul and the Supersoul. Paramātmā is the controller, and the *ātmā* is the controlled; therefore they are in different categories. Because the Paramātmā fully cooperates with the *ātmā,* He is known as the constant companion of the living being.

The all-pervading feature of the Lord—which exists in all circumstances of waking and sleeping as well as in potential states and from which the *jīva-śakti* (living force) is generated as both conditioned and liberated souls—is known as Brahman. Since the Lord is the origin of both Paramātmā and Brahman, He is the origin of all living entities and all else that exists. One who knows this engages himself at once in the devotional service of the Lord. Such a pure and fully cognizant devotee of the Lord is fully attached to Him in heart and soul, and whenever such a devotee assembles with similar devotees, they have no engagement but the glorification of the Lord's transcendental activities. Those who are not as perfect as the pure devotees—namely, those who have realized only the Brahman or Paramātmā features of the Lord—cannot appreciate the activities of the perfect devotees. The Lord always helps the pure devotees by imparting necessary knowledge within their hearts, and thus out of His special favor He dissipates all the darkness of ignorance. The speculative philosophers and *yogīs* cannot imagine this, because they more or less depend on their own strength. As stated in the *Kaṭha Upaniṣad* (1.2.23), the Lord can be known only by those whom He favors, and not by anyone else. Such special favors are bestowed upon His pure devotees only. *Śrī Īśopaniṣad* thus points to the favor of the Lord, which is beyond the purview of the *brahmajyoti.*

Mantra Seventeen

वायुरनिलममृतमथेदं भस्मान्तं शरीरम् ।
ॐ क्रतो स्मर कृतं स्मर क्रतो स्मर कृतं स्मर ॥ १७ ॥

vāyur anilam amṛtam
athedaṁ bhasmāntaṁ śarīram
oṁ krato smara kṛtaṁ smara
krato smara kṛtaṁ smara

vāyuḥ—air of life; *anilam*—total reservoir of air; *amṛtam*—indestructible; *atha*—now; *idam*—this; *bhasmāntam*—after being turned to ashes; *śarīram*—body; *oṁ*—O Lord; *krato*—O enjoyer of all sacrifices; *smara*—please remember; *kṛtam*—all that has been done by me; *smara*—please remember; *krato*—O supreme beneficiary; *smara*—please remember; *kṛtam*—all that I have done for You; *smara*—please remember.

TRANSLATION

Let this temporary body be burnt to ashes, and let the air of life be merged with the totality of air. Now, O my Lord, please remember all my sacrifices, and because You are the ultimate beneficiary, please remember all that I have done for You.

PURPORT

The temporary material body is certainly a foreign

dress. The *Bhagavad-gītā* (2.20) clearly says that after the destruction of the material body the living entity is not annihilated, nor does he lose his identity. The identity of the living entity is never impersonal or formless; on the contrary, it is the material dress that is formless and that takes a shape according to the form of the indestructible person. No living entity is originally formless, as is wrongly thought by those with a poor fund of knowledge. This *mantra* verifies the fact that the living entity exists after the annihilation of the material body.

In the material world, material nature displays wonderful workmanship by creating varieties of bodies for the living beings according to their propensities for sense gratification. The living entity who wants to taste stool is given a material body that is quite suitable for eating stool—that of a hog. Similarly, one who wants to eat the flesh and blood of other animals may be given a tiger's body equipped with suitable teeth and claws. But the human being is not meant for eating flesh, nor does he have any desire to taste stool, even in the most aboriginal state. Human teeth are so made that they can chew and cut fruit and vegetables, although there are two canine teeth so that primitive humans can eat flesh if they so desire.

But in any case, the material bodies of all animals and men are foreign to the living entity. They change according to the living entity's desire for sense gratification. In the cycle of evolution, the living entity changes bodies one after another. When the world was full of water, the living entity took an aquatic form. Then he passed to vegetable life, from vegetable life to worm life, from worm life to bird life, from bird life to animal life, and from animal life to the human form. The highest developed form is this human form when it is possessed of a full sense of spiritual knowledge. The highest development of one's spiritual sense is described in this *mantra:* One should give up the material body, which will be turned to ashes, and allow the air of life to merge into the eternal reservoir of air. The living being's activities are performed within the body through the movements of different kinds of air, known in summary as *prāṇa-vāyu.* The *yogīs* generally study how to control the airs of the body. The soul is supposed to rise from one circle of air to another until it rises to the *brahma-randhra,* the highest circle. From that point the perfect *yogī* can transfer himself to any planet he likes. The process is to give up one material body and then enter into another. But the highest perfection of such changes occurs only when the living entity is able to give up the material body altogether, as suggested in this *mantra,* and enter into the spiritual atmosphere, where he can develop a completely different type of body—a spiritual body, which never has to meet death or change.

Here in the material world, material nature forces the living entity to change his body due to his different desires for sense gratification. These desires are represented in the various species of life, from germs to the most perfected material bodies, those of Brahmā and the demigods. All of these living entities have bodies composed of matter in different shapes. The intelligent man sees oneness not in the variety of the bodies but in the spiritual identity. The spiritual spark, which is part and parcel of the Supreme Lord, is the same whether he is in a body of a hog or in the body of a demigod. The living entity takes on different bodies according to his pious and vicious activities. The human body is highly developed and has full consciousness. According to the *Bhagavad-gītā* (7.19), the most perfect man surrenders unto the Lord after many, many lifetimes of culturing knowledge. The culture of knowledge reaches perfection only when the knower comes to the point of surrendering unto the Supreme Lord, Vāsudeva. Otherwise, even after attaining knowledge of one's spiritual identity, if one does not come to the point of knowing that the living entities are eternal parts and parcels of the whole and can never become the whole, one has to fall down again into the material atmosphere. Indeed, one must fall down even if he has become one with the *brahmajyoti.*

As we have learned from previous *mantras,* the *brahmajyoti* emanating from the transcendental body of the Lord is full of spiritual sparks that are individual entities with the full sense of existence. Sometimes these living entities want to enjoy their senses, and therefore they are placed in the material world to become false lords under the dictation of the senses. The desire for lordship is the material disease of the living being, for under the spell of sense enjoyment he transmigrates through the various bodies manifested in the material world. Becoming one with the *brahmajyoti* does not represent mature knowledge. Only by surrendering unto the Lord completely and developing one's sense of spiritual service does one reach the highest perfectional stage.

In this *mantra* the living entity prays to enter the spiritual kingdom of God after relinquishing his material body and material air. The devotee prays to the Lord to remember his activities and the sacrifices he has performed before his material body is turned into ashes. He makes this prayer at the time of death, with full consciousness of his past deeds and of the ultimate goal. One who is completely under the rule of material nature remembers the heinous activities he performed during the existence of his material body, and consequently he gets another material body after death. The *Bhagavad-gītā* (8.6) confirms this truth:

yaṁ yaṁ vāpi smaran bhāvaṁ
tyajaty ante kalevaram
taṁ tam evaiti kaunteya
sadā tad-bhāva-bhāvitaḥ

"Whatever state of being one remembers when he quits his body, O son of Kuntī, that state he will attain without fail." Thus the mind carries the living entity's propensities into the next life.

Unlike the simple animals, who have no developed mind, the dying human being can remember the activities of his life like dreams at night; therefore his mind remains surcharged with material desires, and consequently he cannot enter into the spiritual kingdom with a spiritual body. The devotees, however, develop a sense of love for Godhead by practicing devotional service to the Lord. Even if at the time of death a devotee does not remember his service to the Lord, the Lord does not forget him. This prayer is given to remind the Lord of the devotee's sacrifices, but even if there is no such reminder, the Lord does not forget the service rendered by His pure devotee.

The Lord clearly describes His intimate relationship with His devotees in the *Bhagavad-gītā* (9.30–34): "Even if one commits the most abominable action, if he is engaged in devotional service he is to be considered saintly because he is properly situated in his determination. He quickly becomes righteous and attains lasting peace. O son of Kuntī, declare it boldly that My devotee never perishes. O son of Pṛthā, those who take shelter in Me, though they be of lower birth—women, *vaiśyas* [merchants] as well as *śūdras* [workers]—can attain the supreme destination. How much more this is so of the righteous *brāhmaṇas,* the devotees and the saintly kings. Therefore, having come to this temporary, miserable world, engage in loving service unto Me. Engage your mind always in thinking of Me, become My devotee, offer obeisances to Me and worship Me. Being completely absorbed in Me, surely you will come to Me."

Śrīla Bhaktivinoda Ṭhākura explains these verses in this way: "One should regard a devotee of Kṛṣṇa to be on the right path of the saints, even though such a devotee may seem to be *su-durācāra,* 'a person of loose character.' One should try to understand the real purport of the word *su-durācāra.* A conditioned soul has to act for double functions—namely for the maintenance of the body and again for self-realization. Social status, mental development, cleanliness, austerity, nourishment and the struggle for existence are all for the maintenance of the body. The self-realization part of one's activities is executed in one's occupation as a devotee of the Lord, and one performs actions in that connection also. One must perform these two different functions along parallel lines, because a conditioned soul cannot give up the maintenance of his body. The proportion of activities for maintenance of the body decreases, however, in proportion to the increase in devotional service. As long as the proportion of devotional service does not come to the right point, there is a chance for an occasional exhibition of worldliness. But it should be noted that such worldliness cannot continue for long because, by the grace of the Lord, such imperfections will come to an end very shortly. Therefore the path of devotional service is the only right path. If one is on the right path, even an occasional occurrence of worldliness does not hamper one in the advancement of self-realization."

The facilities of devotional service are denied the impersonalists because they are attached to the *brahmajyoti* feature of the Lord. As suggested in the previous *mantras,* they cannot penetrate the *brahmajyoti* because they do not believe in the personality of Godhead. Their business is mostly word jugglery and mental speculation. Consequently the impersonalists pursue a fruitless labor, as confirmed in the Twelfth Chapter of the *Bhagavad-gītā* (12.5).

All the facilities suggested in this *mantra* can be easily obtained by constant contact with the personal feature of the Absolute Truth. Devotional service to the Lord consists essentially of nine transcendental activities: (1) hearing about the Lord, (2) glorifying the Lord, (3) remembering the Lord, (4) serving the lotus feet of the Lord, (5) worshiping the Lord, (6) offering prayers to the Lord, (7) serving the Lord, (8) enjoying friendly association with the Lord, and (9) surrendering everything unto the Lord. These nine principles of devotional service—taken altogether or one by one—help a devotee remain constantly in touch with God. In this way, at the end of life it is easy for the devotee to remember the Lord. By adopting only one of these nine principles, the following renowned devotees of the Lord were able to achieve the highest perfection: (1) By hearing of the Lord, Mahārāja Parīkṣit, the hero of *Śrīmad-Bhāgavatam,* attained the desired result. (2) Just by glorifying the Lord, Śukadeva Gosvāmī, the speaker of *Śrīmad-Bhāgavatam,* attained his perfection. (3) By praying to the Lord, Akrūra attained the desired result. (4) By remembering the Lord, Prahlāda Mahārāja attained the desired result. (5) By worshiping the Lord, Pṛthu Mahārāja attained perfection. (6) By serving the lotus feet of the Lord, the goddess of fortune, Lakṣmī, attained perfection. (7) By rendering personal service to the Lord, Hanumān attained the desired result. (8) Through his friendship with the Lord, Arjuna attained the desired result. (9) By surrendering everything he had to the Lord, Mahārāja Bali attained the desired result.

Actually, the explanation of this *mantra* and of practically all the *mantras* of the Vedic hymns is summarized in the *Vedānta-sūtra* and properly explained in *Śrīmad-Bhāgavatam. Śrīmad-Bhāgavatam* is the mature fruit of the Vedic tree of wisdom. In *Śrīmad-Bhāgavatam* this particular *mantra* is explained in the questions and answers between Mahārāja Parīkṣit and Śukadeva Gosvāmī at the very beginning of their meeting. Hearing and chanting of the science of God is the basic principle of devotional life. The complete *Bhāgavatam* was heard by Mahārāja Parīkṣit and chanted by Śukadeva Gosvāmī. Mahārāja Parīkṣit inquired from Śukadeva because Śukadeva was a greater spiritual master than any great *yogī* or transcendentalist of his time.

Mahārāja Parīkṣit's main question was: "What is the duty of every man, specifically at the time of death?" Śukadeva Gosvāmī answered:

tasmād bhārata sarvātmā
bhagavān īśvaro hariḥ
śrotavyaḥ kīrtitavyaś ca
smartavyaś cecchatābhayam

"Everyone who desires to be free from all anxieties should always hear about, glorify and remember the Personality of Godhead, who is the supreme director of everything, the extinguisher of all difficulties, and the Supersoul of all living entities." (*Bhāg.* 2.1.5)

So-called human society is generally engaged at night in sleeping and having sex and during the daytime in earning as much money as possible or else in shopping for family maintenance. People have very little time to talk about the Personality of Godhead or to inquire about Him. They have dismissed God's existence in so many ways, primarily by declaring Him to be impersonal, that is, without sense perception. But in the Vedic literature—whether the *Upaniṣads*, *Vedānta-sūtra, Bhagavad-gītā* or *Śrīmad-Bhāgavatam*—it is declared that the Lord is a sentient being and is supreme over all other living entities.

His glorious activities are identical with Himself. One should therefore not indulge in hearing and speaking of the rubbish activities of worldly politicians and so-called big men in society but should mold his life in such a way that he can engage in godly activities without wasting a second. *Śrī Īśopaniṣad* directs us toward such godly activities.

Unless one is accustomed to devotional practice, what will he remember at the time of death, when the body is dislocated, and how can he pray to the almighty Lord to remember his sacrifices? Sacrifice means denying the interest of the senses. One has to learn this art by employing the senses in the service of the Lord during one's lifetime. One can utilize the results of such practice at the time of death.

Mantra Eighteen

अग्ने नय सुपथा राये अस्मान् विश्वानि देव वयुनानि विद्वान्।
युयोध्यस्मज्जुहुराणमेनो भूयिष्ठां ते नमउक्तिं विधेम ॥ १८ ॥

agne naya supathā rāye asmān
viśvāni deva vayunāni vidvān
yuyodhy asmaj juhurāṇam eno
bhūyiṣṭhāṁ te nama-uktiṁ vidhema

agne—O my Lord, as powerful as fire; *naya*—kindly lead; *supathā*—by the right path; *rāye*—for reaching You; *asmān*—us; *viśvāni*—all; *deva*—O my Lord; *vayunāni*—actions; *vidvān*—the knower; *yuyodhi*—kindly remove; *asmat*—from us; *juhurāṇam*—all hindrances on the path; *enaḥ*—all vices; *bhūyiṣṭhām*—most numerous; *te*—unto You; *namaḥ-uktim*—words of obeisance; *vidhema*—I do.

TRANSLATION

O my Lord, as powerful as fire, O omnipotent one, now I offer You all obeisances, falling on the ground at Your feet. O my Lord, please lead me on the right path to reach You, and since You know all that I have done in the past, please free me from the reactions to my past sins so that there will be no hindrance to my progress.

PURPORT

By surrendering to the Lord and praying for His causeless mercy, the devotee can progress on the path of complete self-realization. The Lord is addressed as fire because He can burn anything into ashes, including the sins of the surrendered soul. As described in the previous *mantras,* the real or ultimate aspect of the Absolute is His feature as the Personality of Godhead, and His impersonal *brahmajyoti* feature is a dazzling covering over His face. Fruitive activities, or the *karma-kāṇḍa* path of self-realization, is the lowest stage in this endeavor. As soon as such activities even slightly deviate from the regulative principles of the *Vedas,* they are transformed into *vikarma,* or acts against the interest of the actor. Such *vikarma* is enacted by the illusioned living entity simply for sense gratification, and thus such activities become hindrances on the path of self-realization.

Self-realization is possible in the human form of life, but not in other forms. There are 8,400,000 species, or forms of life, of which the human form qualified by brahminical culture presents the only chance to obtain knowledge of transcendence. Brahminical culture includes truthfulness, sense control, forbearance, simplicity, full knowledge and full faith in God. It is not that one simply becomes proud of his high parentage. Just as being born the son of a big man affords one a chance to become a big man, so being born the son of a *brāhmaṇa* gives one a chance to become a *brāhmaṇa.* But such a birthright is not everything, for one still has to attain the brahminical qualifications for himself. As soon as one becomes proud of his birth as the son of a *brāhmaṇa* and neglects to acquire the qualifications of a real *brāhmaṇa,* he at once becomes degraded and falls from the path of self-realization. Thus his life's mission as a human being is defeated.

In the *Bhagavad-gītā* (6.41–42) we are assured by the Lord that the *yoga-bhraṣṭas,* or souls fallen from the path of self-realization, are given a chance to rectify themselves by taking birth either in the families of good *brāhmaṇas* or in the families of rich merchants. Such births afford higher chances for self-realization. If these chances are misused due to illusion, one loses the good opportunity of human life afforded by the almighty Lord.

The regulative principles are such that one who follows them is promoted from the platform of fruitive activities to the platform of transcendental knowledge. After many, many lifetimes of cultivating transcendental knowledge, one becomes perfect when he surrenders unto the Lord. This is the general procedure. But one who surrenders at the very beginning, as recommended in this *mantra,* at once surpasses all preliminary stages simply by adopting the devotional attitude. As stated in the *Bhagavad-gītā* (18.66), the Lord at once takes charge of such a surrendered soul and frees him from all the reactions to his sinful acts. There are many sinful reactions involved in *karma-kāṇḍa* activities, whereas in *jñāna-kāṇḍa,* the path of philosophical development, the number of such sinful activities is smaller. But in devotional service to the Lord, the path of *bhakti,* there is practically no chance of incurring sinful reactions. One who is a devotee of the Lord attains all the good qualifications of the Lord Himself, what to speak of those of a *brāhmaṇa*. A devotee automatically attains the qualifications of an expert *brāhmaṇa* authorized to perform sacrifices, even though the devotee may not have taken his birth in a *brāhmaṇa* family. Such is the omnipotence of the Lord. He can make a man born in a *brāhmaṇa* family as degraded as a lowborn dog-eater, and He can also make a lowborn dog-eater superior to a qualified *brāhmaṇa* simply on the strength of devotional service.

Since the omnipotent Lord is situated within the heart of everyone, He can give directions to His sincere devotees by which they can attain the right path. Such directions are especially offered to the devotee, even if he desires something else. As far as others are concerned, God gives sanction to the doer only at the risk of the doer. But in the case of a devotee, the Lord directs him in such a way that he never acts wrongly. The *Śrīmad-Bhāgavatam* (11.5.42) says:

sva-pāda-mūlaṁ bhajataḥ priyasya
tyaktānya-bhāvasya hariḥ pareśaḥ
vikarma yac cotpatitaṁ kathañcid
dhunoti sarvaṁ hṛdi sanniviṣṭaḥ

"The Lord is so kind to the devotee who is fully surrendered to His lotus feet that even though the devotee sometimes falls into the entanglement of *vikarma*—acts against the Vedic directions—the Lord at once rectifies such mistakes from within his heart. This is because the devotees are very dear to the Lord."

In this *mantra* of *Śrī Īśopaniṣad,* the devotee prays to the Lord to rectify him from within his heart. To err is human. A conditioned soul is very often apt to commit mistakes, and the only remedial measure to take against such unintentional sins is to give oneself up to the lotus feet of the Lord so that He may guide one to avoid such pitfalls. The Lord takes charge of fully surrendered souls; thus all problems are solved simply by surrendering oneself unto the Lord and acting in terms of His directions. Such directions are given to the sincere devotee in two ways: one is by way of the saints, scriptures and spiritual master, and the other is by way of the Lord Himself, who resides within the heart of everyone. Thus the devotee, fully enlightened with Vedic knowledge, is protected in all respects.

Vedic knowledge is transcendental and cannot be understood by mundane educational procedures. One can understand the Vedic *mantras* only by the grace of the Lord and the spiritual master (*yasya deve parā bhaktir yathā deve tathā gurau*). If one takes shelter of a bona fide spiritual master, it is to be understood that he has obtained the grace of the Lord. The Lord appears as the spiritual master for the devotee. Thus the spiritual master, the Vedic injunctions and the Lord Himself from within—all guide the devotee in full strength. In this way there is no chance for a devotee to fall again into the mire of material illusion. The devotee, thus protected all around, is sure to reach the ultimate destination of perfection. The entire process is hinted at in this *mantra,* and *Śrīmad-Bhāgavatam* (1.2.17–20) explains it further:

Hearing and chanting the glories of the Lord is

itself an act of piety. The Lord wants everyone to hear and chant His glories because He is the well-wisher of all living entities. By hearing and chanting the glories of the Lord, one becomes cleansed of all undesirable things, and then one's devotion becomes fixed upon the Lord. At this stage the devotee acquires the brahminical qualifications, and the effects of the lower modes of nature (passion and ignorance) completely vanish. The devotee becomes fully enlightened by virtue of his devotional service, and thus he comes to know the path of the Lord and the way to attain Him. As all doubts diminish, he becomes a pure devotee.

Thus end the Bhaktivedanta Purports to Śrī Īśopaniṣad, *the knowledge that brings one nearer to the Supreme Personality of Godhead, Kṛṣṇa.*

Appendixes

About the Author

His Divine Grace A. C. Bhaktivedanta Swami Prabhupāda appeared in this world in 1896 in Calcutta, India. He first met his spiritual master, Śrīla Bhaktisiddhānta Sarasvatī Gosvāmī, in Calcutta in 1922. Bhaktisiddhānta Sarasvatī, a prominent religious scholar and the founder of sixty-four Gauḍīya Maṭhas (Vedic institutes) in India, liked this educated young man and convinced him to dedicate his life to teaching Vedic knowledge. Śrīla Prabhupāda became his student and, in 1933, his formally initiated disciple.

At their first meeting Śrīla Bhaktisiddhānta Sarasvatī requested Śrīla Prabhupāda to broadcast Vedic knowledge in English. In the years that followed, Śrīla Prabhupāda wrote a commentary on the *Bhagavad-gītā,* assisted the Gauḍīya Maṭha in its work, and, in 1944, started *Back to Godhead,* an English fortnightly magazine. Single-handedly, Śrīla Prabhupāda edited it, typed the manuscripts, checked the galley proofs and even distributed the individual copies. The magazine is now being continued by his disciples in the West.

In 1950 Śrīla Prabhupāda retired from married life, adopting the *vānaprastha* (retired) order to devote more time to his studies and writing. He traveled to the holy city of Vṛndāvana, where he lived in humble circumstances in the historic temple of Rādhā-Dāmodara. There he engaged for several years in deep study and writing. He accepted the renounced order of life (*sannyāsa*) in 1959. At Rādhā-Dāmodara, Śrīla Prabhupāda began work on his life's masterpiece: a multivolume commentated translation of the eighteen-thousand-verse *Śrīmad-Bhagavatam* (*Bhāgavata Purāṇa*). He also wrote *Easy Journey to Other Planets.*

After publishing three volumes of the *Bhāgavatam,* Śrīla Prabhupāda came to the United States, in September 1965, to fulfill the mission of his spiritual master. Subsequently, His Divine Grace wrote more than fifty volumes of authoritative commentated translations and summary studies of the philosophical and religious classics of India.

When he first arrived by freighter in New York City, Śrīla Prabhupāda was practically penniless. Only after almost a year of great difficulty did he establish the International Society for Krishna Consciousness, in July of 1966. Before he passed away on November 14, 1977, he had guided the Society and seen it grow to a worldwide confederation of more than one hundred *āśramas,* schools, temples, institutes, and farm communities.

In 1972 His Divine Grace introduced the Vedic system of primary and secondary education in the West by founding the *gurukula* school in Dallas, Texas. Since then his disciples have established similar schools throughout the United States and the rest of the world.

Śrīla Prabhupāda also inspired the construction of several large international cultural centers in India. The center at Śrīdhāma Māyāpur is the site for a planned spiritual city, an ambitions project for which construction will extend over many years to come. In Vṛndāvana are the magnificent Kṛṣṇa-Balarāma Temple and International Guesthouse, *gurukula* school and Śrīla Prabhupāda Memorial and Museum. There is also a major cultural and educational center in Bombay. Major centers are planned in Delhi, Bangalore and in a dozen other important locations on the Indian subcontinent.

Śrīla Prabhupāda's most significant contribution, however, is his books. Highly respected by scholars for their authority, depth and clarity, they are used as textbooks in numerous college courses. His writings have been translated into over fifty languages. The Bhaktivedanta Book Trust, established in 1972 to publish the works of His Divine Grace, has thus become the world's largest publisher of books in the field of Indian religion and philosophy.

In just twelve years, despite his advanced age, Śrīla Prabhupāda circled the globe fourteen times on lecture tours that took him to six continents. Yet this vigorous schedule did not slow his prolific literary output. His writings constitute a veritable library of Vedic philosophy, religion, literature and culture.

Kṛṣṇa Consciousness at Home

From what we've read in *Śrī Īśopaniṣad,* it's clear how important it is for everyone to practice Kṛṣṇa consciousness, devotional service to Lord Kṛṣṇa. Of course, living in the association of Kṛṣṇa's devotees in a temple or *āśrama* makes it easier to practice devotional service. But if you're determined, you can follow at home the teachings of Kṛṣṇa consciousness and thus convert your home into a temple.

Spiritual life, like material life, means practical activity. The difference is that whereas we perform material activities for the benefit of ourselves or those we consider ours, we perform spiritual activities for the benefit of Lord Kṛṣṇa, under the guidance of the scriptures and the spiritual master. The key is to accept the guidance of the scripture and the *guru.* Kṛṣṇa declares in the *Bhagavad-gītā* that a person can achieve neither happiness nor the supreme destination of life—going back to Godhead, back to Lord Kṛṣṇa—if he or she does not follow the injunctions of the scriptures. And *how* to follow the scriptural rules by engaging in practical service to the Lord—that is explained by a bona fide spiritual master. Without following the instructions of a spiritual master who is in an authorized chain of disciplic succession coming from Kṛṣṇa Himself, we cannot make spiritual progress. The practices outlined here are the timeless practices of *bhakti-yoga* as given by the foremost spiritual master and exponent of Kṛṣṇa consciousness in our time, His Divine Grace A. C. Bhaktivedanta Swami Prabhupāda, founder-*ācārya* of the International Society for Krishna Consciousness (ISKCON).

The purpose of spiritual knowledge is to bring us closer to God, or Kṛṣṇa. Kṛṣṇa says in the *Bhagavad-gītā* (18.55), *bhaktyā māṁ abhijānāti:* "I can be known only by devotional service." Knowledge guides us in proper action. Spiritual knowledge directs us to satisfy the desires of Kṛṣṇa through practical engagements in His loving service. Without practical application, theoretical knowledge is of little value.

Spiritual knowledge is meant to direct us in all aspects of life. So we should try to organize our lives in such a way as to follow Kṛṣṇa's teachings as far as possible. We should try to do our best, to do more than is simply convenient. Then it will be possible for us to rise to the transcendental plane of Kṛṣṇa consciousness, even while living far from a temple.

Chanting Hare Kṛṣṇa

The first principle in devotional service is to chant the Hare Kṛṣṇa *mahā-mantra* (*mahā* means "great"; *mantra* means "sound that liberates the mind from ignorance"):

Hare Kṛṣṇa, Hare Kṛṣṇa, Kṛṣṇa Kṛṣṇa, Hare Hare
Hare Rāma, Hare Rāma, Rāma Rāma, Hare Hare

You can chant these holy names of the Lord anywhere and at any time, but it is best to set a specific time of the day to regularly chant. Early morning hours are ideal.

The chanting can be done in two ways: singing the *mantra*, called *kīrtana* (usually done in a group), and saying the *mantra* to oneself, called *japa* (which literally means "to speak softly"). Concentrate on hearing the sound of the holy names. As you chant, pronounce the names clearly and distinctly, addressing Kṛṣṇa in a prayerful mood. When your mind wanders, bring it back to the sound of the Lord's names. Chanting is a prayer to Kṛṣṇa that means "O energy of the Lord [Hare], O all-attractive Lord [Kṛṣṇa], O Supreme Enjoyer [Rāma], please engage me in Your service." The more attentively and sincerely you chant these names of God, the more spiritual progress you will make.

Since God is all-powerful and all-merciful, He has kindly made it very easy for us to chant His names, and He has also invested all His powers in them. Therefore the names of God and God Himself are identical. This means that when we chant the holy names of Kṛṣṇa and Rāma we are directly associating with God and being purified. Therefore we should always try to chant with devotion and reverence. The Vedic literature states that Lord Kṛṣṇa is personally dancing on your tongue when you chant His holy name.

When you chant alone, it is best to chant on *japa* beads (available from the Bhaktivedanta Book Trust, at one of the addresses given in the advertisement at the end of this book). This not only helps you fix your attention on the holy name, but it also helps you count the number of times you chant the *mantra* daily. Each strand of *japa* beads contains 108 small beads and one large bead, the head bead. Begin on a bead next to the head bead and gently roll it between the thumb and middle finger of your right hand as you chant the full Hare Kṛṣṇa *mantra.* Then move to the next bead and repeat the process. In this way, chant on each of the 108 beads until you reach the head bead again. This is one round of *japa*. Then, without chanting on the head bead, reverse the beads and start your second round on the last bead you chanted on.

Initiated devotees vow before the spiritual master to chant at least sixteen rounds of the Hare Kṛṣṇa *mantra* daily. But even if you can chant only one round a day, the principle is that once you commit yourself to chanting that round, you should try to complete it every day without fail. When you feel you can chant more, then increase the minimum number of rounds you chant each day—but don't fall below that number. You can chant more than your fixed number, but you should maintain a set minimum each day. (Please note that the beads are sacred and therefore should never touch the ground or be put in an unclean place. To keep your beads clean, it's best to carry them in a special bead bag, also available from the Bhaktivedanta Book Trust.)

Aside from chanting *japa,* you can also sing the Lord's holy names in *kīrtana*. While you can sing alone, *kīrtana* is generally performed with others. A melodious *kīrtana* with family or friends is sure to enliven everyone. ISKCON devotees use traditional melodies and instruments, especially in the temple, but you can chant to any melody and use any musical instruments to accompany your chanting. As Lord Caitanya said, "There are no hard and fast rules for chanting Hare Kṛṣṇa." One thing you might want to do, however, is order some *kīrtana* and *japa* audiotapes from the Bhaktivedanta Book Trust.

Setting Up Your Altar

You'll likely find that *japa* and *kīrtana* are more effective when done before an altar. Lord Kṛṣṇa and His pure devotees are so kind that they allow us to worship them even through their pictures. It's something like mailing a letter: You can't mail a letter by placing it in just any box; you must use the mailbox authorized by the government. Similarly, we cannot imagine a picture of God and worship that, but we can worship the authorized picture of God, and Kṛṣṇa accepts our worship through that picture.

Setting up an altar at home means receiving the Lord and His pure devotees as your most honored guests. Where should you set up the altar? Well, how would you seat a guest? An ideal place would be clean, well lit, and free from drafts and household disturbances. Your guest, of course, would need a comfortable chair, but for the picture of Kṛṣṇa's form a wall shelf, a mantelpiece, a corner table, or the top shelf of a bookcase will do. You wouldn't seat a guest in your home and then ignore him; you'd provide a place for yourself to sit, too, where you could comfortably face him and enjoy his company. So don't make your altar inaccessible.

What do you need to set up your altar? Here are the essentials:

1. A picture of Śrīla Prabhupāda.
2. A picture of Lord Caitanya and His associates.
3. A picture of Śrī Śrī Rādhā-Kṛṣṇa.

In addition, you may want an altar cloth, water cups (one for each picture), candles with holders, a special plate for offering food, a small bell, incense, an incense holder, and fresh flowers, which you may offer in vases or simply place before each picture. If you're interested in more elaborate Deity worship, ask any of the ISKCON devotees or write to the Bhaktivedanta Book Trust.

The first person we worship on the altar is the spiritual master. The spiritual master is not God. Only God is

God. But because the spiritual master is His dearmost servant, God has empowered him, and therefore he deserves the same respect as that given to God. He links the disciple with God and teaches him the process of *bhakti-yoga.* He is God's ambassador to the material world. When a president sends an ambassador to a foreign country, the ambassador receives the same respect as that accorded the president, and the ambassador's words are as authoritative as the president's. Similarly, we should respect the spiritual master as we would God, and revere his words as we would His.

There are two main kinds of *gurus:* the instructing *guru* and the initiating *guru.* Everyone who takes up the process of *bhakti-yoga* as a result of coming in contact with ISKCON owes an immense debt of gratitude to Śrīla Prabhupāda. Before Śrīla Prabhupāda left India in 1965 to spread Kṛṣṇa consciousness abroad, almost no one outside India knew anything about the practice of pure devotional service to Lord Kṛṣṇa. Therefore, everyone who has learned of the process through his books, his *Back to Godhead* magazine, his tapes, or contact with his followers should offer respect to Śrīla Prabhupāda. As the founder and spiritual guide of the International Society for Krishna Consciousness, he is the instructing *guru* of us all.

As you progress in *bhakti-yoga,* you may eventually want to accept initiation. Before he left this world in 1977, Śrīla Prabhupāda authorized a system in which advanced and qualified devotees would carry on his work by initiating disciples in accordance with his instructions. At present there are many spiritual masters in ISKCON. To learn how you can get in touch with them for spiritual guidance, ask a devotee at your nearby temple, or write to the president of one of the ISKCON centers listed at the end of this book.

The second picture on your altar should be one of the *pañca-tattva,* Lord Caitanya and His four leading associates. Lord Caitanya is the incarnation of God for this age. He is Kṛṣṇa Himself, descended in the form of His own devotee to teach us how to surrender to Him, specifically by chanting His holy names and performing other activities of *bhakti-yoga.* Lord Caitanya is the most merciful incarnation, for He makes it easy for anyone to attain love of God through the chanting of the Hare Kṛṣṇa *mantra.*

And of course your altar should have a picture of the Supreme Personality of Godhead, Lord Śrī Kṛṣṇa, with His eternal consort, Śrīmatī Rādhārāṇī. Śrīmatī Rādhārāṇī is Kṛṣṇa's spiritual potency. She is devotional service personified, and devotees always take shelter of Her to learn how to serve Kṛṣṇa.

You can arrange the pictures in a triangle, with the picture of Śrīla Prabhupāda on the left, the picture of Lord Caitanya and His associates on the right, and the picture of Rādhā and Kṛṣṇa (slightly larger than the others, if possible) on a small raised platform behind and in the center. Or you can hang the picture of Rādhā and Kṛṣṇa on the wall above the altar.

Carefully clean the altar each morning. Cleanliness is essential in Deity worship. Remember, you wouldn't neglect to clean the room of an important guest, and when you establish an altar you invite Kṛṣṇa and His pure devotees to reside as the most exalted guests in your home. If you have water cups, rinse them out and fill them with fresh water daily. Then place them conveniently close to the pictures. You should remove flowers in vases as soon as they're slightly wilted, or daily if you've offered them at the base of the pictures. You should offer fresh incense at least once a day, and, if possible, light candles and place them near the pictures when you're chanting before the altar.

Please try the things we've suggested so far. It's very simple, really: If you try to love God, you'll gradually realize how much He loves you. That's the essence of *bhakti-yoga.*

Prasādam: How to Eat Spiritually

By His immense transcendental energies, Kṛṣṇa can convert matter into spirit. If we place an iron rod in a fire, before long the rod becomes red hot and acts just like fire. In the same way, food prepared for and offered to Kṛṣṇa with love and devotion becomes spiritualized. Such food is called Kṛṣṇa *prasādam,* which means "the mercy of Lord Kṛṣṇa."

Eating *prasādam* is a fundamental practice of *bhakti-yoga.* In other forms of *yoga* one must artificially repress the senses, but the *bhakti-yogī* can engage his or her senses in a variety of pleasing spiritual activities, such as tasting delicious food offered to Lord Kṛṣṇa. In this way the senses gradually become spiritualized and bring the devotee more and more transcendental pleasure by being engaged in devotional service. Such spiritual pleasure far surpasses any kind of material experience.

Lord Caitanya said of *prasādam,* "Everyone has tasted these foods before. However, now that they have been prepared for Kṛṣṇa and offered to Him with devotion, these foods have acquired extraordinary tastes and uncommon fragrances. Just taste them and see the difference in the experience! Apart from the taste, even the fragrance pleases the mind and makes one forget any other fragrance. Therefore one should know that the spiritual nectar of Kṛṣṇa's lips must have touched these ordinary foods and imparted to them all their transcendental qualities."

Eating only food offered to Lord Kṛṣṇa is the perfection of vegetarianism. In itself, being a vegetarian is not enough; after all, even pigeons and monkeys are vegetarians. But when we go beyond vegetarianism to a diet of *prasādam,* our eating becomes helpful in achieving the goal of human life—reawakening the soul's original relationship with God. In the *Bhagavad-gītā* Kṛṣṇa says that unless one eats only food that has been offered to Him in sacrifice, one will suffer the reactions of *karma.*

How to Prepare and Offer Prasādam

As you walk down the supermarket aisles selecting the foods you will offer to Kṛṣṇa, you need to know what is offerable and what is not. In the *Bhagavad-gītā,* Lord Kṛṣṇa states, "If one offers Me with love and devotion a leaf, a flower, a fruit, or water, I will accept it." From this verse it is understood that we can offer Kṛṣṇa foods prepared from milk products, vegetables, fruits, nuts, and grains. (Write to the Bhaktivedanta Book Trust for one of the many Hare Kṛṣṇa cookbooks.) Meat, fish, and eggs are not offerable. And a few vegetarian items are also forbidden—garlic and onions, for example, which are in the mode of darkness. (*Hing,* or asafetida, is a tasty substitute for them in cooking and is available at most Indian groceries or from the Bhaktivedanta Book Trust.) Nor can you offer to Kṛṣṇa coffee or tea that contain caffeine. If you like these beverages, purchase caffeine-free coffee and herbal teas.

While shopping, be aware that you may find meat, fish, and egg products mixed with other foods; so be sure to read labels carefully. For instance, some brands of yogurt and sour cream contain gelatin, a substance made from the horns, hooves, and bones of slaughtered animals. Also, make sure the cheese you buy contains no rennet, an enzyme extracted from the stomach tissues of slaughtered calves. Most hard cheese sold in America contains rennet, so be careful about any cheese you can't verify as rennetless.

Also avoid foods cooked by nondevotees. According to the subtle laws of nature, the cook acts upon the food not only physically but mentally as well. Food thus becomes an agent for subtle influences on your consciousness. The principle is the same as that at work with a painting: a painting is not simply a collection of strokes on a canvas but an expression of the artist's state of mind, which affects the viewer. So if you eat food cooked by nondevotees—employees working in a factory, for example—then you're sure to absorb a dose of materialism and *karma*. So as far as possible use only fresh, natural ingredients.

In preparing food, cleanliness is the most important principle. Nothing impure should be offered to God; so keep your kitchen very clean. Always wash your hands thoroughly before entering the kitchen. While preparing food, do not taste it, for you are cooking the meal not for yourself but for the pleasure of Kṛṣṇa. Arrange portions of the food on dinnerware kept especially for this purpose; no one but the Lord should eat from these dishes. The easiest way to offer food is simply to pray, "My dear

Lord Kṛṣṇa, please accept this food," and to chant each of the following prayers three times while ringing a bell (see the Sanskrit Pronunciation Guide on page 104):

1. Prayer to Śrīla Prabhupāda:

nama oṁ viṣṇu-pādāya kṛṣṇa-preṣṭhāya bhū-tale
śrīmate bhaktivedānta-svāmin iti nāmine

namas te sārasvate deve gaura-vāṇī-pracāriṇe
nirviśeṣa-śūnyavādi-pāścātya-deśa-tāriṇe

"I offer my respectful obeisances unto His Divine Grace A. C. Bhaktivedanta Swami Prabhupāda, who is very dear to Lord Kṛṣṇa, having taken shelter at His lotus feet. Our respectful obeisances are unto you, O spiritual master, servant of Bhaktisiddhānta Sarasvatī Gosvāmī. You are kindly preaching the message of Lord Caitanyadeva and delivering the Western countries, which are filled with impersonalism and voidism."

2. Prayer to Lord Caitanya:

namo mahā-vadānyāya kṛṣṇa-prema-pradāya te
kṛṣṇāya kṛṣṇa-caitanya-nāmne gaura-tviṣe namaḥ

"O most munificent incarnation! You are Kṛṣṇa Himself appearing as Śrī Kṛṣṇa Caitanya Mahāprabhu. You have assumed the golden color of Śrīmatī Rādhārāṇī, and You are widely distributing pure love of Kṛṣṇa. We offer our respectful obeisances unto You."

3. Prayer to Lord Kṛṣṇa:

namo brahmaṇya-devāya go-brāhmaṇa-hitāya ca
jagad-dhitāya kṛṣṇāya govindāya namo namaḥ

"I offer my respectful obeisances unto Lord Kṛṣṇa, who is the worshipable Deity for all *brāhmaṇas*, the well-wisher of the cows and the *brāhmaṇas,* and the benefactor of the whole world. I offer my repeated obeisances to the Personality of Godhead, known as Kṛṣṇa and Govinda."

Remember that the real purpose of preparing and offering food to the Lord is to show your devotion and gratitude to Him. Kṛṣṇa accepts your devotion, not the physical offering itself. God is complete in Himself—He doesn't need anything—but out of His immense kindness He allows us to offer food to Him so that we can develop our love for Him.

After offering the food to the Lord, wait at least five minutes for Him to partake of the preparations. Then you should transfer the food from the special dinnerware and wash the dishes and utensils you used for the offering. Now you and any guests may eat the *prasādam.* While you eat, try to appreciate the spiritual value of the food. Remember that because Kṛṣṇa has accepted it, it is nondifferent from Him, and therefore by eating it you will become purified.

Everything you offer on your altar becomes *prasādam,* the mercy of the Lord. The flowers, the incense, the water, the food—everything you offer for the Lord's pleasure becomes spiritualized. When we offer the Lord something with genuine love and devotion, He enters into the offering, and thus the remnants are nondifferent from Him. So you should not only deeply respect the things you've offered, but you should distribute them to others as well. Distribution of *prasādam* is an essential part of Deity worship.

Everyday Life: The Four Regulative Principles

Anyone serious about progressing in Kṛṣṇa consciousness must try to avoid the following four sinful activities:

1. **Eating meat, fish, or eggs.** These foods are saturated with the modes of passion and ignorance and therefore cannot be offered to the Lord. A person who eats these foods participates in a conspiracy of violence against helpless animals and thus stops his spiritual progress dead in its tracks.

2. **Gambling.** Gambling invariably puts one into anxiety and fuels greed, envy, and anger.

3. **The use of intoxicants.** Drugs, alcohol, and tobacco, as well as any drink or food containing caffeine, cloud the mind, overstimulate the senses, and make it impossible to follow the principles of *bhakti-yoga*.

4. **Illicit sex.** This is extramarital sex or sex in marriage for reasons other than procreation. Sex for pleasure compels one to identify with the body and takes one far from Kṛṣṇa consciousness. The scriptures teach that sex is the most powerful force binding us to the material world. Anyone serious about advancing in Kṛṣṇa consciousness should minimize sex or eliminate it entirely.

Engagement in Practical Devotional Service

Everyone must do some kind of work, but if you work only for yourself you must accept the karmic reactions of that work. As Lord Kṛṣṇa says in the *Bhagavad-gītā* (3.9), "Work done as a sacrifice for Viṣṇu [Kṛṣṇa] has to be performed. Otherwise work binds one to the material world."

You needn't change your occupation, except if you're now engaged in a sinful job such as working as a butcher or bartender. If you're a writer, write for Kṛṣṇa; if you're an artist, create for Kṛṣṇa; if you're a secretary, type for Kṛṣṇa. You may also directly help the temple in your spare time, and you should sacrifice some of the fruits of your work by contributing a portion of your earnings to help maintain the temple and propagate Kṛṣṇa consciousness. Some devotees living outside the temple buy Hare Kṛṣṇa literature and distribute it to their friends and associates, or they engage in a variety of services at the temple. There is also a wide network of devotees who gather in each other's homes for chanting, worship, and study. Write to your local temple or the Society's secretary to learn of any such programs near you.

Additional Devotional Principles

There are many more practices that will help you become Kṛṣṇa conscious. Here are two vital ones:

Studying Hare Kṛṣṇa literature. Śrīla Prabhupāda, the founder-*ācārya* of ISKCON, dedicated much of his time to writing books such as the *Śrīmad-Bhāgavatam,* the source of the chapter describing the fate of the sinful family man. Hearing the words—or reading the writings—of a realized spiritual master is an essential spiritual practice. So try to set aside some time every day to read Śrīla Prabhupāda's books. You can get a free catalog of available books and tapes from the Bhaktivedanta Book Trust.

Associating with devotees. Śrīla Prabhupāda established the Hare Kṛṣṇa movement to give people in general the chance to associate with devotees of the Lord. This is the best way to gain faith in the process of Kṛṣṇa consciousness and become enthusiastic in devotional service. Conversely, maintaining intimate connections with nondevotees slows one's spiritual progress. So try to visit the Hare Kṛṣṇa center nearest you as often as possible.

In Closing

The beauty of Kṛṣṇa consciousness is that you can take as much as you're ready for. Kṛṣṇa Himself promises in the *Bhagavad-gītā* (2.40), "There is no loss or diminution in this endeavor, and even a little advancement on this path protects one from the most fearful type of danger." So bring Kṛṣṇa into your daily life, and we guarantee you'll feel the benefit.

Hare Kṛṣṇa!

References

The purports of *Śrī Īśopaniṣad* are all confirmed by standard Vedic authorities. The following authentic scriptures are cited in this volume. For specific page references, consult the general index.

Atharva Veda

Bhagavad-gītā

Bhakti-rasāmṛta-sindhu

Brahma-saṁhitā

Gopāla-tāpanī Upaniṣad

Hari-bhakti-sudhodaya

Kaṭha Upaniṣad

Mahābhārata

Mahā Upaniṣad

Mokṣa-dharma

Muṇḍaka Upaniṣad

Nārāyaṇa Upaniṣad

Ṛg Veda

Śrīmad-Bhāgavatam

Varāha Upaniṣad

Vedānta-sūtra

Viṣṇu Purāṇa

Glossary

A

Ācārya—a spiritual master; one who teaches by example.
Adhīra—one who is disturbed by material illusion.
Akarma—action that frees one from the cycle of birth and death.
Amara—deathless.
Ānanda—the Supreme Lord's aspect of bliss.
Ananta—unlimited.
Anumāna—inductive reasoning.
Apāpa-viddha—pure and uncontaminated.
Aparā prakṛti—the inferior energy of the Lord.
Apauruṣeya—not delivered by any mundane person.
Arcā-vigraha—the form of God manifested through material elements, as in a painting or statue of Kṛṣṇa worshiped in a temple or home. In this form the Lord personally accepts worship from His devotees.
Āroha—the ascending process of knowledge.
Asura—a demon.
Ātmā—the self (the body, the mind, the intellect, the Supersoul or the individual soul).
Ātma-hā—a killer of the soul.
Avidyā—ignorance.
Avyakta—the unmanifested stage of creation.

B

Bhagavān—the Supreme Personality of Godhead, possessor of all opulences.
Bhaktas—devotees of Śrī Kṛṣṇa.
Brahmajyoti—the effulgence emanating from the body of the Supreme Lord, which illuminates the spiritual world.

Brāhmaṇa—a person wise in Vedic knowledge, fixed in goodness, and knowledgeable of Brahman, the Absolute Truth; a member of the first Vedic social order.
Buddha—learned.

C

Cit—the Supreme Lord's aspect of knowledge.

D

Dhīra—one who is not disturbed by material illusion.
Dvija-bandhu—one born in a *brāhmaṇa* family but not qualified as a *brāhmaṇa.*

G

Guru—a spiritual master.

I

Īśāvāsya—the god-centered conception.

J

Jīva-śakti—the living force.
Jñāna—knowledge; the culture of knowledge.

K

Kaniṣṭha-adhikārī—a person in the lowest stage of realization of God.
Karma—material, fruitive activity and its reactions; also, fruitive actions performed in accordance with Vedic injunctions.
Karma-bandhana—work that binds one to the material world.
Karma-yoga—offering the fruit of one's work to Kṛṣṇa.
Karmīs—those engaged in activities of sense gratification.
Kṣatriya(s)—a warrior or administrator; the second Vedic social order.

M

Madhyama-adhikārīs—those in the intermediate stage of God realization.

Mahā-bhāgavata—a great personality who sees everything in relation to the Supreme Lord.

Māyā—illusion; accepting something that is not.

Māyayāpahṛta-jñānas—those whose knowledge has been stolen by illusion.

Mṛtyuloka—the place of death, the material world.

Mūḍhas—fools or asses.

N

Naiṣkarmya—*See: Akarma*

Narādhama—the lowest of human beings.

Nirguṇa—without material qualities.

P

Param brahma—the supreme spirit, i.e., the Supreme Lord, Kṛṣṇa.

Paramparā—the line of disciplic succession.

Parā prakṛti—the superior energy of the Lord.

Parā śakti—*See: Parā prakṛti*

Pitās—forefathers.

Prāṇa-vāyu—the subtle airs in the body; also, the movements of these airs.

Prasāda—food spiritualized by being offered to Kṛṣṇa.

Pratyakṣa—direct evidence.

S

Sac-cid-ānanda-vigraha—an eternal form full of knowledge and bliss.

Saguṇa—with qualities.

Sat—the Supreme Lord's aspect of eternity.

Śrīmat—a *vaiśya;* a member of the mercantile community.

Śruti—knowledge via hearing; also, the original Vedic

scriptures (the *Vedas* and *Upaniṣads*), given directly by the Supreme L ord.

Śuci—a spiritually advanced *brāhmaṇa.*

Śuddha—antiseptic.

Śūdras—the worker class in society.

Śukra—omnipotent.

Sura—a godly person.

T

Tri-pād-vibhūti—the spiritual nature, which is three fourths of the Lord's energy.

U

Uttama-adhikārī—a person in the highest stage of God realization.

V

Vaikuṇṭhalokas—the planets in the spiritual sky.

Vaiśya—a farmer or merchant; the third Vedic social order.

Varṇāśrama—the Vedic social system of four social and four spiritual orders.

Veda—knowledge.

Vedas—the original revealed scriptures, first spoken by the Lord Himself.

Veda-vāda-ratas—those who give their own explanations of the *Vedas.*

Vidyā—knowledge.

Vikarma—sinful work, performed against scriptural injunctions.

Viṣṇu-tattva—a plenary portion of the Supreme Lord.

Y

Yoga-bhraṣṭa—a soul fallen from the path of self-realization.

Sanskrit Pronunciation Guide

Throughout the centuries, the Sanskrit language has been written in a variety of alphabets. The mode of writing most widely used throughout India, however, is called *devanāgarī,* which means, literally, the writing used in "the cities of the demigods." The *devanāgarī* alphabet consists of forty-eight characters: thirteen vowels and thirty-five consonants. Ancient Sanskrit grammarians arranged this alphabet according to practical linguistic principles, and this order has been accepted by all Western scholars. The system of transliteration used in this book conforms to a system that scholars in the last fifty years have accepted to indicate the pronunciation of each Sanskrit sound.

Vowels

अ a आ ā इ i ई ī उ u ऊ ū ऋ ṛ

ॠ ṝ ऌ ḷ ए e ऐ ai ओ o औ au

Consonants

Gutturals:	क ka	ख kha	ग ga	घ gha	ङ ṅa
Palatals:	च ca	छ cha	ज ja	झ jha	ञ ña
Cerebrals:	ट ṭa	ठ ṭha	ड ḍa	ढ ḍha	ण ṇa
Dentals:	त ta	थ tha	द da	ध dha	न na
Labials:	प pa	फ pha	ब ba	भ bha	म ma
Semivowels:	य ya	र ra	ल la	व va	
Sibilants:		श śa	ष ṣa	स sa	
Aspirate:	ह ha	Anusvāra	ं ṁ	Visarga:	ः ḥ

Sanskrit Pronunciation Guide

Numerals

०-0 १-1 २-2 ३-3 ४-4 ५-5 ६-6 ७-7 ८-8 ९-9

The vowels are written as follows when pronounced after a consonant:

ा ā ि i ी ī ु u ू ū ृ ṛ ॄ ṝ े e ै ai ो o ौ au

For example: क ka का kā कि ki की kī कु ku कू kū

कृ kṛ कॄ kṝ के ke कै kai को ko कौ kau

Generally two or more consonants in conjunction are written together in a special form, as for example: क्ष kṣa त्र tra

The vowel "**a**" is implied after a consonant with no vowel symbol.

The symbol *virāma* (्) indicates that there is no final vowel: क्

The vowels are pronounced as follows:

a – as in but
ā – as in far but held twide as long as **a**
ai – as in aisle
au – as in how
e – as in they
i – as in pin
ī – as in pique but held twice as long as **i**
ḷ – as in **lree**
o – as in **go**
ṛ – as in **rim**
ṝ – as in **reed** but held twice as long as **ṛ**
u – as in push
ū – as in rule but held twice as long as **u**

The consonants are pronounced as follows:

Gutturals
(pronounced from the throat)
k – as in **k**ite
kh – as in Ec**kh**art
g – as in **g**ive
gh – as in di**g-h**ard
ṅ – as in si**n**g

Labials
(pronounced with the lips)
p – as in **p**ine
ph – as in u**p-h**ill (not f)
b – as in **b**ird
bh – as in ru**b-h**ard
m – as in **m**other

Cerebrals
(pronounced with tip of tongue against roof of mouth)
ṭ – as in **t**ub
ṭh – as in ligh**t-h**eart
ḍ – as in **d**ove
ḍh – as in re**d-h**ot
ṇ – as in si**n**g

Dentals
(pronounced as cerebrals but with tongue against teeth)
t – as in **t**ub
th – as in ligh**t-h**eart
d – as in **d**ove
dh – as in re**d-h**ot
n – as in **n**ut

Aspirate
h – as in **h**ome

Anusvāra
ṁ – a resonant nasal sound like in the French word *bo***n**

Palatals
(pronounced with middle of tongue against palate)
c – as in **ch**air
ch – as in staun**ch-h**eart
j – as in **j**oy
jh – as in he**dgeh**og
ñ – as in ca**ny**on

Semivowels
y – as in **y**es
r – as in **r**un
l – as in **l**ight
v – as in **v**ine, except when preceded in the same syllable by a consonant, then like in s**w**an

Sibilants
ś – as in the German word *sprechen*
ṣ – as in **sh**ine
s – as in **s**un

Visarga
ḥ – a final **h**-sound: **aḥ** is pronounced like **aha**; **iḥ** like **ihi**

In Sanskrit there is no strong accentuation of syllables or pausing between words in a line, but only a flowing of short and long syllables. The long syllables, which are held twice as long as the short ones, are those whose vowel is long (**ā, ai, au, e, ī, o, ṝ, ū**) or whose short vowel is followed by more than one consonant (including **ḥ** and **ṁ**). Aspirated consonants (those followed by an **h**) count as single consonants.

Index of Sanskrit Verses

This index constitutes a complete listing of the first and third lines of each of the Sanskrit verses of *Śrī Īśopaniṣad,* arranged in English alphabetical order. In the first column the Sanskrit transliteration is given, and in the second and third columns respectively the *mantra* number and page number for each verse are to be found.

Index of Verses Quoted

This index lists the verses quoted in the purports of *Śrī Īśopaniṣad*. Numerals in boldface type refer to the first or third lines of verses quoted in full; numerals in roman type refer to partially quoted verses.

General Index

Numerals in boldface type indicate references to translations of the verses of *Śrī Īśopaniṣad.*

Hare Krishna Centers In North America, Australia, & New Zealand

NORTH AMERICA

CANADA

Montreal, Quebec — 1626 Pie IX Boulevard, H1V 2C5/ Tel. (514) 521-1301
Ottawa, Ontario — 212 Somerset St. E., K1N 6V4/ Tel. (613) 565-6544
Regina, Saskatchewan — 1279 Retallack St., S4T 2H8/ Tel. (306) 525-1640
Toronto, Ontario — 243 Avenue Rd., M5R 2J6/ Tel. (416) 922-5415
Vancouver, B.C. — 5462 S.E. Marine Dr., Burnaby V5J 3G8/ Tel. (604) 433-9728

FARM COMMUNITY

Ashcroft, B.C. — Saranagati Dhama, Box 99, Ashcroft, B.C. V0K 1A0

RESTAURANTS

Hamilton, Ontario — Govinda's, 195 Locke St. South, L8T 4B5/ Tel. (416) 523-6209
Ottawa — (at ISKCON Ottawa)
Toronto — Hare Krishna Dining Room (at ISKCON Toronto)
Vancouver — Hare Krishna Buffet (at ISKCON Vancouver)
Vancouver — The Hare Krishna Place, 46 Begbie St., New Westminster

U.S.A.

Atlanta, Georgia — 1287 South Ponce de Leon Ave. N.E., 30306/ Tel. (404) 378-9234
Baltimore, Maryland — 200 Bloomsbury Ave., Catonsville, 21228/ Tel. (410) 744-1624 or 4069
Boise, Idaho — 1615 Martha St., 83706/ Tel. (208) 344-4274
Boston, Massachusetts — 72 Commonwealth Ave., 02116/ Tel. (617) 247-8611
Boulder, Colorado — 917 Pleasant St., 80302/ Tel. (303) 444-7005
Chicago, Illinois — 1716 W. Lunt Ave., 60626/ Tel. (312) 973-0900
Cleveland, Ohio — 11206 Clifton Blvd., 44102/ Tel. (216) 651-6670
Dallas, Texas — 5430 Gurley Ave., 75223/ Tel. (214) 827-6330
Denver, Colorado — 1400 Cherry St., 80220/ Tel. (303) 333-5461
Detroit, Michigan — 383 Lenox Ave., 48215/ Tel. (313) 824-6000
Gainesville, Florida — 214 N.W. 14th St., 32603/ Tel. (904) 336-4183
Gurabo, Puerto Rico — Route 181, P.O. Box 8440 HC-01, 00778-9763/ Tel. (809) 737-5222
Hartford, Connecticut — 1683 Main St., E. Hartford, 06108/ Tel. (203) 289-7252
Honolulu, Hawaii — 51 Coelho Way, 96817/ Tel. (808) 595-3947
Houston, Texas — 1320 W. 34th St., 77018/ Tel. (713) 686-4482
Laguna Beach, California — 285 Legion St., 92651/ Tel. (714) 494-7029
Lansing, Michigan — 1914 E. Michigan Ave., 48912/ Tel. (517) 484-2209
Long Island, New York — 197 S. Ocean Ave., Freeport, 11520/ Tel. (516) 867-9045
Los Angeles, California — 3764 Watseka Ave., 90034/ Tel. (310) 836-2676
Miami, Florida — 3220 Virginia St., 33133/ Tel. (305) 442-7218
New Orleans, Louisiana — 2936 Esplanade Ave., 70119/ Tel. (504) 484-6084
New York, New York — 305 Schermerhorn St., Brooklyn, 11217/ Tel. (718) 855-6714
New York, New York — 26 Second Avenue, 10003/ Tel. (212) 420-8803
Philadelphia, Pennsylvania — 51 West Allens Lane, 19119/ Tel. (215) 247-4600
Philadelphia, Pennsylvania — 529 South St., 19147/ Tel. (215) 829-0077
St. Louis, Missouri — 3926 Lindell Blvd., 63108/ Tel. (314) 535-8085
San Diego, California — 1030 Grand Ave., Pacific Beach, 92109/ Tel. (619) 483-2500
San Francisco, California — 84 Carl St.,94117/ Tel. (415) 661-7320
San Francisco, California — 2334 Stuart St., Berkeley, 94705/ Tel. (510) 644-1113
Seattle, Washington — 1420 228th Ave. S.E., Issaquah, 98027/ Tel. (206) 391-3293
Tallahassee, Florida — 1323 Nylic St. (mail: P.O. Box 20224, 32304)/ Tel. (904) 681-9258
Topanga, California — 20395 Callon Dr., 90290/ Tel. (213) 455-1658
Towaco, New Jersey — (mail: P.O. Box 109, 07082)/ Tel. (201) 299-0970
Tucson, Arizona — 711 E. Blacklidge Dr., 85719/ Tel. (602) 792-0630
Walla Walla, Washington — 314 E. Poplar, 99362/ Tel. (509) 525-7133
Washington, D.C. — 10310 Oaklyn Dr., Potomac, Maryland 20854/ Tel. (301) 299-2100

FARM COMMUNITIES

Alachua, Florida (New Ramana-reti) — Box 819, Alachua, 32615/ Tel. (904) 462-2017
Carriere, Mississippi (New Talavan) — 31492 Anner Road, 39426/ Tel. (601) 798-6623

Gurabo, Puerto Rico (New Govardhana Hill) — (contact ISKCON Gurabo)
Hillsborough, North Carolina (New Goloka) — Rt. 6, Box 701, 27278/ Tel. (919) 732-6492
Mulberry, Tennessee (Murari-sevaka) — Rt. No. 1, Box 146-A, 37359/ Tel (615) 759-6888
Port Royal, Pennsylvania (Gita Nagari) — R.D. No. 1, Box 839, 17082/ Tel. (717) 527-4101

RESTAURANTS AND DINING

Atlanta — The Hare Krishna Dinner Club (at ISKCON Atlanta)
Boise — Govinda's, 500 W. Main St./ Tel. (208) 338-9710
Chicago — Govinda's Buffet (at ISKCON Chicago)
Dallas — Kalachandji's (at ISKCON Dallas)
Denver — Govinda's (at ISKCON Denver)
Detroit — Govinda's (at ISKCON Detroit)/ Tel. (313) 331-6740
Eugene, Oregon — Govinda's Vegetarian Buffet, 270 W. 8th St., 97401/ Tel. (503) 686-3531
Honolulu — Gauranga's Vegetarian Dining (at ISKCON Honolulu)
Laguna Beach, California — Gauranga's (at ISKCON Laguna Beach)
Lansing, Michigan — Govinda's Diners' Club (at ISKCON Lansing)
Los Angeles — Govinda's, 9624 Venice Blvd., Culver City, 90230/ Tel. (310) 836-1269
Miami — (at ISKCON Miami)
Ojai, California — Govinda's Veggie Buffet, 1002 E. Ojai Ave., 93023/ Tel. (805) 646-1133
Philadelphia — Govinda's, 521 South Street, 19147/ Tel. (215) 829-0077
Provo, Utah — Govinda's Buffet, 260 North University, 84601/ Tel. (801) 375-0404
St. Louis, Missouri — Govinda's (at ISKCON St. Louis)
San Diego — Govinda's at the Beach (at ISKCON San Diego)/ Tel (619) 483-5266
San Francisco — Govinda's (at ISKCON Berkeley)/ Tel. (510) 644-2777
Tucson, Arizona — Govinda's (at ISKCON Tucson)

AUSTRALIA, NEW ZEALAND

Adelaide, Australia — 74 Semaphore Rd., Semaphore, S. A. 5019/ Tel. +61 (08) 493 200
Brisbane, Australia — 95 Bank Rd., Graceville, Q.L.D. (mail: P.O. Box 83, Indooroopilly 4068)/ Tel. +61 (07) 379-5455
Canberra, Australia — P.O Box 1411, Canberra ACT 2060/ Tel. +61 (06) 290-1869
Christchurch, New Zealand — 83 Bealey Ave. (mail: P.O. Box 25-190 Christchurch)/ Tel. +64 (03) 3665-174
Melbourne, Australia — 197 Danks St., Albert Park, Victoria 3206 (mail: P.O. Box 125)/ Tel. +61 (03) 699-5122
Perth, Australia — 144 Railway Parade (cnr. The Strand), Bayswater (mail: P.O. Box 102, Bayswater, W. A. 6053)/ Tel. +61 (09) 370-1552
Sydney, Australia — 180 Falcon St., North Sydney, N.S.W. 2060 (mail: P. O. Box 459, Cammeray, N.S.W. 2062)/ Tel. (02) 959-4558
Wellington, New Zealand — 6 Shotter St., Karori (mail: P.O. Box 2753, Wellington)/ Tel. +64 (04) 764-445

FARM COMMUNITIES

Auckland, New Zealand (New Varshan) — Hwy. 18, Riverhead, next to Huapai Golf Course (mail: R.D. 2, Kumeu, Auckland)/ Tel. +64 (09) 4128075
Bambra, Australia (New Nandagram) — Oak Hill, Dean's Marsh Road, Bambra, VIC 3241/ Tel. +61 (052) 88-7383
Millfield, Australia — New Gokula Farm, Lewis Lane (off Mt.View Rd. Millfield near Cessnock), N.S.W. (mail: P.O. Box 399, Cessnock 2325, N.S.W., Australia)/ Tel. +61 (049) 98-1800
Murwillumbah, Australia (New Govardhana) — Tyalgum Rd., Eungella, via Murwillumbah N. S. W. 2484 (mail: P.O. Box 687)/ Tel. +61 (066) 72-1903

RESTAURANTS

Auckland, New Zealand — Gopal's, Civic House (1st floor), 291 Queen St./ Tel. +64 (09) 3034885
Brisbane, Australia — Govinda's, 1st _oor, 99 Elizabeth Street/ Tel. +61 (07) 210-0255
Christchurch, New Zealand — Gopal's, 143 Worcester St./ Tel. +64 (03) 3667-035
Melbourne, Australia — Crossways, 1st _oor, 123 Swanston St., Melbourne, Victoria 3000/ Tel. +61 (03) 6502939
Melbourne, Australia — Gopal's, 139 Swanston St., Melbourne, Victoria 3000/ Tel. +61 (03) 650-1578
Perth, Australia — Hare Krishna Food for Life, 200 William St., Northbridge, WA 6003/ Tel. +61 (09) 22716
Sydney, Australia — Govinda's Upstairs and Govinda's Take-Away, 112 Darlinghurst Rd., Darlinghurst, N.S.W. 2010/ Tel. +61 (02) 380-5162
Sydney, Australia — Gopal's (at ISKCON Sydney)